END MATTER

Index of Titles

Outro

The Loss Adjusters are at all times woeful: an inherent disposition confirmed by their close proximity to Portland stone. This material's attitude, a dignified restraint, has calmly developed during more than 150 million years of formation, concentrated on an island off Britain's Dorset coast. Everything that flourished here in the Jurassic period, vital and fully expanded, ultimately perished, became compacted and compressed under the mass of new existence until solidification preserved the remains and finally transformed them into Portland stone.

This stone has absorbed an enormous quantity of death, a sense of which may be transmitted to those who are close to it, if they are vigilant. Fully receptive and woebegone, the Loss Adjusters attempt to quantify the manifold losses associated with Portland and the mortality it is formed of. Through this process, in their estimation, the stone is physically comprised of the demise of prehistorical eras. Metaphorically it embraces the death of the individuals and events it is shaped to memorialise. Practically it sustains the displacement of large portions of its own mass. Additionally, the wider company of Adjusters investigate many incidents and objects worldwide. In general a loss is adjusted for, to their satisfaction, when counterbalanced by a presence. Those working on Portland, however, can be forgiven for jiggering and tweaking their findings to attend to the magnitude of its absences.

The manner in which they interpret loss adjustment is, at the outset, bureaucratic. Crucially, however, the more experienced Adjusters are expected to elaborate on their findings, to expand their frame of reference into a para-academic arena. From there they venture towards quasi-metaphysical speculation. This work, as they see it, has advanced from administration to a realm of critical thinking. What they extravagantly term as the *supersensible* object of their enquiry is something we will return to later.

On Portland they work at No. 52 Easton Street. This is the main street running through the village of Easton, at the centre of the island. Their windows are blacked out and the lights inside emit only a low glow. The rooms are mainly green, with minty pastel walls and olive carpets accompanied by a pervading odour of damp, so that the entire space smells and appears vaguely bilious, or irradiated. Some of the walls are oddly panelled with strips of peeling woodgrain-effect paper veneer. The front and back offices are equipped with desks and chairs along with several cabinets, files and boxes. All these containers are empty with enough dust to suggest — to those who do not look closely — that they have been unused for a while. And yet the central office hosts large printers and photocopiers; turned on but inactive. This windowless area includes a rectangular mirror, carefully screwed in at an angle so that it reflects the room's apparent redundancy, straight on.

At any one time a minimum of five Adjusters are employed. Ostensibly this number ensures that if two need to leave a room, or to venture out for a site trip, they can be accompanied by another, whilst the remaining two stay in each other's vicinity. This measure is an indicator of their need for the mutual affirmation of their existence. One pair are situated in the front office and three in the rear. More Adjusters can be called upon in case of an emergency. At short notice these auxiliary Adjusters will abandon their private activities and hasten to work. They take up their positions and assist in whatever task is demanded of them. Believers, and fully trained, they are able to undertake any of the duties normally assumed by the full-time Adjusters. In the central, windowless office, meetings are held, although here there are no desks or chairs amidst the peripheral hardware devices. The need to stand, they've concluded, also keeps the mind alert, reducing the chances of losing consciousness, the consequence of which would be a fellow Adjuster not being perceived, equating ultimately to a disappearance. During the destabilising conjectures of their gatherings, the Adjusters hold hands. Some of them find the low hum, indicative of the reproductive capacity of the printers and copiers, reassuring.

Their projects are meticulously recorded, filed away, not as physical paperwork, but in their collective minds. Together they agree on how this theoretical filing is grouped into areas of interest. Included under the heading *The Reformulation of Absence as a Sensually Engaged Experience*, for example, is a series of catalogued investigations into materiality. This makes for dubious evidence, attempting as it does to amount to confirmation that individuals, in the midst of a vanishing physical environment, might adjust to this loss by heightening their sensual experiences. There are interviews with lifelong quarrymen, *the agents of stone removal*; who reveal that their engagement with the process of displacement is counterbalanced by the sensual characteristics of their work. The men's statements, fixed in the Adjusters' minds, reveal that they not only live and breathe the stone and its dust, but the effect of long term and intensive exposure to the island's raw matter means that they develop and embody a rich and particular knowledge.

It is the Loss Adjusters' conceit to embellish these accounts with supplementary reflections. These observations leap from factual descriptions, through hypothesis, to a determination that as the quarrymen traverse the stone, work on it and think about it, their perceptions are consistently fused with the awareness of what was there before. It is concluded that these men get the measure of the terrain, not via the immediacy of the land there, but rather by way of the stone that is elsewhere; an experiential understanding that is discerned and documented in the Loss Adjusters' imagined files.

Additional data on *Sensually Engaged Absences* endeavours to encompass explicit bodily encounters. These are evaluations that seek to uncover any evidence of extensive sexual fantasising on the island, that is a result of the displacement of actual corporeal engagements. It is by means of an anonymous survey that this particular assessment is conducted, devoid of facts that might identify the specific location, age or occupation of the respondent, but replete with protracted accounts and descriptive detail. When they meet to assess their progress on the subject, the Loss Adjusters gather in the windowless printing room amidst the gentle drone of the hardware. They acknowledge that in many of the graphic interactions that are imagined, it seems possible to replace the experience of touch and to conjure feelings of ecstasy without any literal engagement. If such experiences are referred to as *transcendental* or *earth-moving* they are cross-referenced with the dossier *On The Supersensible Object*, details of which conclude this section.

One of the fundamental questions the Loss Adjusters ask is how the reality of the stone that is displaced can be sustained on the island. For example, they use photography to make a positive assessment on how the stone's loss can be made manifest. At any time three Loss Adjusters might be found on a field trip, mapping the topology and taking photographs of the quarried land and of the buildings made from it on the island and beyond. Crucially they create material copies, actually printing the maps and the photographs of the construction of houses and spaces across Portland's disrupted landscape. They are sent photographs taken by other Adjusters who record parts of Portland found in different locations (especially London). They then counterpoise their own images of holes with those of buildings such as the National Gallery, the British Museum and the Bank of England. These printed documents, maintained on the island in their offices at No. 52 Easton Street, are material compensation for what is elsewhere, or in their mental records. When taking these photographs, they are keen to recapture what stone they can, whether it is strewn across beaches or scattered on farms, excavated from quarries, processed and reformulated in diverse manifestations, from simple gravestones, to St Paul's Cathedral, from everyday patios and pavements, to the Cenotaph on Whitehall, for example.

A special meeting was convened to witness the filing of their most recent photograph: the Portland stone sculptures on the octagonal capitals underneath Blackfriars Bridge in the City of London. Anyone who walks along this bridge and stops at the recess on the northwest side, can kneel on the curved stone bench and proceed to look over the edge to have their gaze returned by John Birnie Philip's spectacular wild-life carvings in the very stone pursued by the Loss Adjusters. In danger of tipping over and falling into the river below, an Adjuster captured the animate form with the creature's eyes looking back fiercely and directly into the camera. The photograph, now safely on record, is inscribed 'Part of Portland, displaced since 1869'.

The Loss Adjusters have an entirely frivolous dossier on the written word as the instigator of the nonappearance of matter, which it would be counterproductive to reiterate here. It is enough to say that it includes a circular file on metaphor, and a subcategory examining coincidences of letter formations with their own interests, such as their reflections on the centre of the word 'stone' being an 'o'.

On a more consequential note, one of their mental dossiers containing extensive and significant research is missing from their communal minds. All that remains is its title in the central registry: *Compensating for the Depletion of Real Things with Fictionality*. None of the current Adjusters worked on this area, consequently whether the files ever actually existed is a matter of speculation, and their supposed contents the subject of much debate. It is assumed the files investigate a tendency for the contemporary mind to engage with things that have only the most fleeting independent existence, or else things that are self-declared fabrications. Their key concern relates to the epistemological and ontological status of fiction itself.

Weekly meetings are now held in which the Adjusters attempt to make strategic decisions about their perceptions of what is real, and what might be a fiction. Here is a summary of their suppositions: Given the ironic detachment and technological sophistication of our age, one missing study might endeavour to establish the mechanisms and strategies readers and listeners use to believe in insubstantial and fantastical things, conjured only through words. They note that what should be a simple exercise is hampered by how we live in our time of profound contingency and instability in terms of our relationship to each other and to the objects around us. This is then part of a wider contemporary condition, but here on Portland, the situation is heightened by the monumental scale of the loss of ground underfoot. It might therefore be a site left acutely vulnerable to fabulists.

Their absent dossier must refer to how people persist in believing, or suspending their disbelief, in fictions. It should summarise how the escalation of fictionality on the island can take on the form of mythology, legend and fable, numerous yarns, novels set on its former, and therefore imagined, landscape, as well as events taking place in what remains of its present. Practical absences appear to leave an excess of room for imaginative conceptualisation about Portland. A profusion of authors and artists have been, and continue to be, drawn to these shores. They delve into the island's cavities, tunnels and crevices, and from here they emerge with a determination to fill the voids with whatever fanciful improvisations they can concoct.

The Adjusters recognise their conjectural conclusions on this matter to be partial and therefore unsatisfactory. The monitoring of the fictive phenomena is in this way generally seen as impossible to pursue and has in any case been superseded by their enquiry *On The Supersensible Object*.

The Supersensible Object is the most compelling of their current avenues of adjustment. The term, which is both a concept and an indicator of form, was discovered by a pioneering Adjuster in the writing of G. W. F. Hegel. At the time of writing, all other activity has been suspended while this object, now taken on by the entire assembly of Adjusters, is pursued. Central to their thinking is the Hegelian suggestion, as they interpret it, that the present world is *vanishing*. Hegel writes that above the *vanishing present world there opens up a permanent beyond*. And it is precisely a sense of the vanishing — understood as the presence of absence — that chimes with their findings on Portland.

According to this logic, it might only be through the engagement with the void of memorialisation that people are able to confront their consciousness of perception, because that is all there is. What is not here is commemorated at the site of its disappearance. The entire island is a Portland stone memorial, carved out and immense, shaped by convicts and quarryman, hacked at and whittled by hand, sliced and dissected by machine, and perceived as an ongoing sculptural production, created by loss. Only when the Loss Adjusters see this object as a determined construction in their consciousness, can it emerge as a singular and impressive formal entity, and this with distinct sculptural qualities appertaining to memorial. The object's indifference to their interpretation lends itself to their negative assessment of its character. In the first instance, they might not perceive the memorial with any certainty. Eventually, it becomes quite definite.

It is the Loss Adjusters' contention that this sculpted island is made meaningful by its absences, as they resonate on the island itself, rather than elsewhere. But even on Portland, locating the absences of the *supersensible* involves finding something that isn't there. As a consequence, the most obvious way to set about this research is to detect signs of the missing objects' effects. This task is made possible by a complementary form. In other words, *the inverted supersensible world* (as they interpret it), is in itself signified by the existence of the *actual world*, just as quarried cavities are the inverse of monuments. These antithetical objects are locked into a reciprocal bond, perpetually reflecting each other as necessary counterparts. The Adjusters look at a building, or a memorial, and think of a hole; when looking at the hole they think of the building. But, so much more than this; what is sweet in the actual world, is sour in the inverted one, hot is cold, good bad and so on. Immoral events in the actual world are acceptable in the inverted one. Evidence of the excessive disturbance of what appears to be everyday reality, is an indicator of the presence of the *supersensible*.

In addition, extended unwritten marginalia indicate what the *supersensible object* is not. It is dependent on absences but adamantly does not equate a lack of substance with any form of transcendentalism, quasi-religious mysticism or spiritualism.

Importantly, the Loss Adjusters acknowledge that *supersensibility* cannot begin to compensate for the devastation of emotional loss or grief. They return frequently to the impossibility of articulating grief and the paradox of the attempt to overcome bereavement by making loss present in stone. This attempt, that is so much the work of sculpture and memorial, is an issue at the heart of their enquiry, but one which is yet to be resolved. Here the process of representation appears transfixed or petrified.

Among the Adjusters there is rumour of a deleted folder which if recovered and opened must be investigated by the entire team. The valiant Adjusters who work in this lacuna must assess the danger that they themselves might be displaced, or cease to be present. According to *the principles of supersensibility*, they must proceed by investigating their consciousness of their own perceptions. And they will begin by asking if it will be possible for their work to continue to exist, should they themselves vanish.

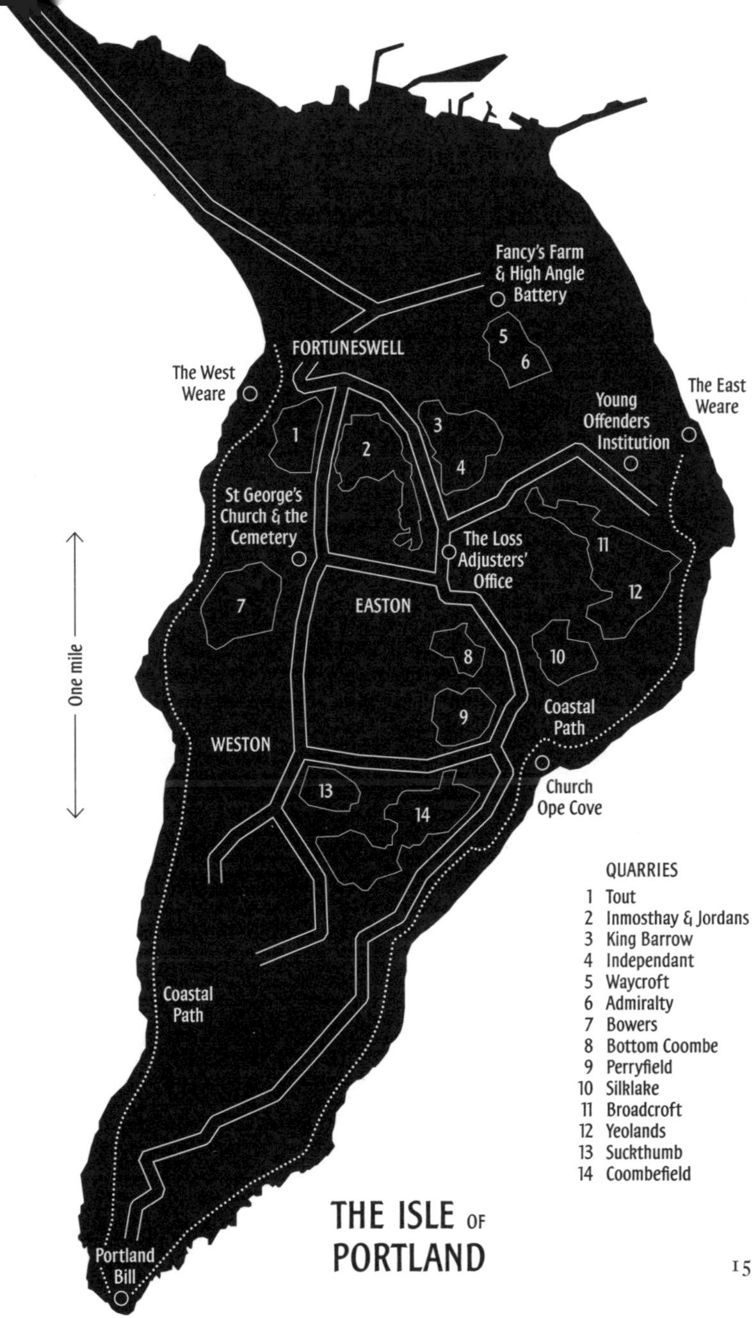

THE ISLE OF PORTLAND

Appendix (a)

Ostensible Format of Loss Adjusters' Report No. _
Retrieved From The Memory Archive
Further to The Loss of *The Writer-In-Residence*

Details of Displacement
Predicaments
Circumstances
Evidence of the Vanishing Present, etc.

It has been drawn to our attention that there has never been a confirmed sighting of the writer who is said to occupy the flat above our offices at No. 52 Easton Street. To date, it has been assumed that she is of advanced years, and rarely leaves the apartment. However, the case provides much indeterminacy for us to dwell upon and we are currently investigating the possibility that she has disappeared.

The flat occupies two floors. First floor consists of one kitchen, one bathroom, one living room. Second floor consists of two bedrooms. All rooms in good condition. Basic furnishings and equipment. Clean. Tidy. As far as it is possible to surmise, the resident's possessions, including a small 24-key electronic keyboard, her clothing and passport, remain in the residence. On the desk: a half-empty mug of coffee, a computer, a voice recorder and a black-and-white postcard depicting the convict quarries. On the computer: a number of files deleted by the writer, which we have subsequently recovered. These are a series of fictions about Portland. Her characters include a young offender turned gravedigger and two sisters named Horrocks — the deviant daughters of a dead quarryman.

Exhibits

Exhibit (a), audio file 1 of 2, discovered on the computer

Transcript of audio file:

> [FOOTSTEPS]
> 'I'm back here again, at Bowers Quarry. There's no one else around. Before it gets dark, I want to record what I witnessed. I know what I saw. It was a man with a wheelbarrow. And in the barrow, there was a body — a dead man.
>
> [FOOTSTEPS STOP]
> 'This is close enough. I'm on the edge, with St George's to my left and the chasm of the quarry directly in front of me. I can't get any closer. There was a body here. I know what I saw. But this place is made all the more disconcerting by the weird combination of banal scrubland and otherworldliness. I mean, it's so ordinary here but also terrible. The prison over there. The church. So many graves here. A terrace of ordinary houses there. I wonder what it would be like to reside in one of them, on the edge of this abyss with the giant holes, the massive rocks and boulders and crevices, the ancientness of it, the lack of living people; it's a moonscape more than a landscape, or a barren future. No, it's not empty. It's an elemental rush of exposed sensual surfaces.

[PAUSE]
'On the far side I can see the clearly demarcated layers of stone, marking time all the way back to the Jurassic age, and at its base, the square entrance to the new mine they're developing. Like many of the other quarries, this one's backed right up to the village borders. But here they've found a way to keep going. They're starting to mine under the roads, the houses and the cricket field. While children scream and run they'll remove the stone from underneath their school playground. And somewhere right here, underground, they're skirting around the cemetery. I'm tired. I need to get back to the writing. I have to delete what I've written so far, the Horrocks' story etc., none of it's right. I shouldn't be here. I'm too old to be scraping around doing this kind of thing.

[CLOTHING RUSTLES]
'What's that? It's just a rabbit. And another. There are so many of them, hopping carefree all around here. I want to be carefree. The little buggers add to the burrowing of course. Portland's so full of cavities, maybe the entire island will succumb and collapse one day. That church tower will lift off, like a rocket from the crypt and the entire isle of Portland will cave in, in its wake.

[PAUSE]
'Okay, this is it. I was standing right here when I saw that young man with the potbellied corpse in the wheelbarrow. I came back the following day and there he was again, but in place of the body, he was pushing a barrow full of stone. I come back regularly and most times I see

him. He's always with the stones. The missing body matter continues to trouble me. It was here.

[INTAKE OF BREATH]
'There he is! He's moving between discarded stones on the far side of the quarry. He's got the wheelbarrow. It's still full of rubble. That must be difficult to manage on this terrain. His face isn't visible beneath his hoodie. I'd swear he had a body the first time I saw him, but now it's not possible to be certain of that either. I have to stop coming here. It's probably better not to know what he's doing, or what he's done. I need to get back to work. And tomorrow, I'll make a fresh start on the writing.'

Attachment

The quarryman had two daughters. Although he raised them to a state of viability, he died disappointed by their failure to flourish. Celestine and Hazeline once strove to do something their father would recognise as worthwhile. By the time they reached their thirties, this sense of ambition had dissipated and their desire to please was behind them. He was a good man, just worried for them, as beyond what he understood of the world, it seemed replete with danger. Unable to progress in their father's profession, the sisters remained in a form of stasis. When he died they changed their names. They sold his house and calculated they could see out their days on Portland, nestled among the stones, living simply and sleeping in their respective workaday huts. Hazeline's was on Church Ope Cove, towards the centre of the island's east coast. Celestine moved to the West Weare, next to Chesil Beach. They chose matching clothes and plaited each other's hair. They planned to settle in a condition of untimeliness, that to others might seem something like a premature death, however the sisters were intensely happy at the prospect.

On the morning Hazeline moved into the hut on Church Ope Cove, she boarded up her front window. This blocked the sea view and beyond that, the mainland's staggering Purbeck peninsula. Although her hut was directly on the beach and saturated by the smells and sounds of the churning water, the mutability of the sea's form was something from which she preferred to avert her eyes. Instead she turned her back and gazed inland.

The land at this very spot at Church Ope is on record as having failed on numerous occasions. The Great Southwell Landslip accounted for the sliding of no less than a mile and a half of Portland, dislodging most of St Andrew's church, its graves and the cadavers they contained, and dispersing them across the cliffside and the cove. With this in mind, and a blade-type screwdriver in hand, she encouraged a small fissure between the boards on the hut's landward wall; an opening that allowed her to peer through and keep a single but keen eye on Portland's terrain. The rock face was partly covered in shrubs, but she had no interest in plant life. At this narrow schism, she crouched and contentedly spied the stone.

On that same morning, Celestine arrived at Chesil Beach, on the other side of Portland. She preferred not to look up at the dramatic aspect of the West Weare, where gigantic loose stones were scattered ominously across the near vertical cliff face that loomed over the huts. Instead she reclined on the cosy bunk inside her cabin. From there she could see through the picture window. Her body, at ease in the nook, rested, immobile, while the view carried her out across the indeterminate sea. Her eyes then wandered along the coastline that seemed independent of the land. The end of this eccentric beach was never visible, which created for her the impression of a highway to oblivion. She loved it.

Later that afternoon Celestine and Hazeline left their huts and walked towards each other, across Portland's quarries; those that were disused, or overgrown, and others simply at downtime. They whispered and wandered in the familiar tunnels of Inmosthay and the filled-in Suckthumb. As was their habit, they sat and talked in the abandoned contours of Broadcroft and King Barrow. Typically, their conversation centred on their deceased father and ranged from there through their histories. Many avenues had been closed to them but they had managed to find their own ways to engage with Portland.

Hazeline stood close to her sister and said, 'I should really have been a quarryman, like Dad and his dad, and all their dads. But I was a girl, so it was never going to work out.'

Celestine said, 'I'm not what was expected.'

'Why the fuck should we be what's expected?' said Hazeline.

With great care Celestine put her arm around her sister's shoulder and said, 'I told Dad, that even if I was a boy, it's unlikely I'd have ended up in the quarries — there's not the work anymore. Nowadays quarrying needs fewer bodies. The new machines are driving even the men out of work.'

Hazeline nodded. 'There was that cousin of ours. He did a few months at Admiralty quarry, then he was laid off. He said it was the end of centuries of tradition. Dad said it was the end of everything.'

'But here we are,' said Celestine.

Hazeline said, 'Remember when I joined the TA and when we took art classes in the evenings? We picked up some practical skills, didn't we? We were really good. He still didn't see us, of course. He couldn't have known what to look for.'

When Hazeline let go of her sister's hand, she placed her palm flat against the stone. 'I have something to confess,' she said. 'After we walked together last week, I carried on and went deeper into the quarry. There were tunnels. I saw shadows and rabbits. I was lost for a while. And when I stepped out into the open air I had a peculiar encounter with two men and a woman who work in Easton. They called themselves Loss Adjusters. When they questioned me they were quite insistent. They wanted to understand who I was and what I was doing here and how it was significant. Things like that, but it was a peculiar investigation.'

'It sounds like they were conducting research — on you of all people, Hazy.'

'Yeah, I had my hand against this stone. I said I wanted to reveal everything.'

'They got it, didn't they? I know they got it. You gave it to them.'

'It was weird, the way they phrased their enquiries. They said that my physicality would need to be nothing short of cosmic to counterbalance the terrible emptiness of the quarry.'

Celestine chuckled. 'Now there's a challenge.'

'One of the men and the female Adjuster stood aside. They appeared to note every detail of the interaction but I couldn't hear what they were saying. The other Adjuster kept talking to me and questioning me with a real probing intensity.

Then having been persistent, he suddenly became less communicative. I watched his face for ages. Watched him looking at me. He just stared at my body so I turned around slowly on the spot to give him a better look. He seemed fascinated with how my feet came into contact with the ground, and when I returned my hands to their former position, pressed into the stone, he gasped and said "Are you responsible, for all this?" '

'You told him, I know you did.'

'Yeah. I told him that I'm stubbornly irresponsible.'

'Ha!'

'He kept on looking, with his mouth open, about to talk or wanting to taste something, wanting more from me. Then he just came right out with it, although in a quieter voice. "What we would give, to see your breasts right now," he said. And I did it because I wanted to. It felt so fucking dirty out there. And my nipples were so cold they were pinching, even with his warm hands rubbing them. I got this overwhelming feeling of being examined but I wanted to be pressed between him and the stone. Then the other Adjusters approached, still studying my responses. Their presence should have put a stop to it all of course, but by that time I had his cock out and was beyond caring!'

Both women were silent for a while, both drawing fingers along the single plaits in their hair until Hazeline said, 'It was confusing in that moment, but completely thrilling. I wanted them all to vanish but I was drawn in by their closeness. No,

I'm over-analysing — I just wanted him inside me, in my mouth, or up inside my body. I wanted much more than he could give me. He said, "There's help to hand." I kneeled in the dirt and got his cock in my mouth. That's when the woman cut in, she said something like this, "You've utterly abandoned yourself. You're empty and limitless. You're simultaneously completely aware and conscious of your physicality, because the stone's being removed from under our feet. It's disappearing. It has been, and is being, cut out and displaced, for centuries. It's destabilising. Isn't it? Is that how you understand it?" I stood up with my sore scraped knees then hitched up my skirt and leaned back.

'There was cold stone against my naked backside. Then they started to work in formation. The second male Adjuster stepped up to my right side, stopped and dropped his trousers. He put one of his legs out to cross mine, but he stayed fixed in that awkward open stride. Then he reached across my body and pressed his palm into my breast. His dick was pointing straight at me so I clutched it, of course I did, although I still kept one hand on the rock behind. The woman, who now stood to my left, took hold of my thigh with both hands. She lifted it up, and I know I'm no waif but it was like she had to support a tremendous weight because she positioned herself with one leg stretched out behind her and the other, closest to me, was bent at the knee to help her arms take the strain. As for my thigh, she managed to haul it towards my chest leaving my lower limb hanging and my body exposed. The three of us were lined up like that, when I noticed the other man, he was just standing there, staring at my hole. I told him to fuck me. And when he did, he was so hard and his movement so rhythmic, it was like he was riveting us all into place and we were coming together, fixed in that contorted arrangement, in relief. There were sharp hard edges of cold stone against my naked backside. The island under my feet was pressing into me and scratching at me from behind.'

Celestine interjected, 'There's a long history of banging and cutting on this island. I hope they thanked you!'

'And then some. They thanked me breathlessly, then very formally and said they'd be in touch. It was weird.'

The sisters hugged. They planned to meet the following day, then returned to their huts.

That evening, a passionate force swept across the island: a full-grown runaway horse galloped southward, with a mind to take the coastal path. Its heavy hooves powered down and into the ground. Possessed by a nonsensical rage, the animal shook not only the stone, but the volatile bed of Kimmeridge clay beneath it.

When the horse approached the ground above her hut at Church Ope, Hazeline saw the slipped rock face shudder. Dust fell. Quickly she dressed and ran out of the hut, climbed the steeply inclined steps, until breathless she ran through the wood and the relics of St Andrew's. She saw horseshoe impressions in the mud. Fresh horseshit on the path. There was no easy way along the coast from here. Anyone or anything passing would have reached the wood then have had to turn back towards the main road. She made her way to street level at Southwell. There she saw the beast from behind, picking up a gallop along the road. It took a left turn that would surely set it back on the coastal path.

Miss Hazeline Horrocks thought of her sister Celestine in her hut beside Chesil on the West Weare. There was no way of knowing what the spooked horse intended, but it was heading south on a trajectory that could take it all the way to the Bill and round to head up the entire length of Portland on the west coast. Hazeline was on foot, but if she dashed directly across the centre of the island, she just might reach Celestine ahead of it.

Hazeline looked at the land.

Celestine watched the sea.

The one looking landward saw movement. The other did not. Nor did she see the horse that raced along the clifftop, hell bent. By the time it reached the West Weare its power was of a sinister intensity. That horse kept running until it dropped, and not a single moment of its existence was registered by Celestine. She failed to notice the gigantic stone that teetered and then fell as the horse passed. The impact of this ancient mass tumbling, hitting others, sending them cascading, all the while accompanied by Hazeline's urgent screams; none of this was enough to alert her.

And neither sister realised that their grandfather's grandfather had carelessly used this very spot as a tip for his quarry's overburden and waste matter. It was his stone, still for centuries, that was now decisively moved. It accumulated speed and its terrible weight finally came down upon Celestine's home. The hut disintegrated.

Hazeline had chased the stone down the incline and had seen and heard an abominable pound and cracking at impact. She now stood and stared at the debris. Throughout that evening she watched the arrival of helicopters, medical teams and lifting equipment. The force required to lever the boulder from the wreckage set it rolling again and it travelled unstoppable until it finally plunged into the sea. The emergency services failed to retrieve it along with what must have been a body pulverised and compressed into its surface. Hazeline imagined the intermingling of corpse and rock. There was no option but to allow that stone to absorb this death. She fell to the ground and lost consciousness.

That night Hazeline made her way back to her hut, trembling as she stepped cautiously across the island's surface. Her plait hung flaccid and forlorn on her shoulder. A red-and-white strip of plastic cordon waved in the wind as a warning of the possible hazard to passersby.

Backstory

The Loss Adjusters currently working at No. 52 Easton Street originally arrived on Portland by steam train in 1952. Their objective was to carry out only preliminary investigations into reported sightings of a Rogue Loss Adjuster. He was the sole member of their cohort on record as having submitted an account so false that it upset their balance sheets and discomposed their carefully maintained unity. Given their interests worldwide, they intended to spend no more than a day on the island, taking notes, making diagrams and gathering intelligence. At the end of that day, they returned to Easton Station, only to discover that the last train had already departed. The passenger rail link to Portland had in fact closed, permanently.

The Adjusters felt themselves compelled to remain on Portland. They were in no way despondent at this prospect as, although they had not yet located the Rogue Adjuster, they had discovered, to their enduring fascination, an abundance of evidence of subversive elemental forces and destabilising influences that required their attention.

Years passed and the source of recent rumours about the Rogue has been identified as a story recovered from among the files that were created and then deleted by their writer-in-residence. A General Meeting has been convened to address the writer's story. The text has been committed to the Adjusters' collective memory and will be recounted during the course of their meeting.

Appendix (b)

Ostensible Format of Loss Adjusters' Minutes
For General Meeting No. _
Retrieved From The Memory Archive
Further to The Loss of *The Rogue Loss Adjuster*
Further to The Discovery of *The Writer-in-Residence's narrative: 'The Rogue and The Carniter'*

This report contains *General Meeting Protocol* and *Points of Referral*
NB: This report may include *Fictional Content*

- Gather in sufficient numbers to be wedged between photocopiers and butted up against printers.
- All available auxiliary Adjusters must join the regulars, forming an assembly to consider an agreed agenda.
- Adjusters contribute in rotating sequence; sharing ideas, but equally, needing physical affirmation, the entire company must move to the centre of the room where hands must be held.
- Make protracted eye contact when speaking.
- Support pertinent lines of enquiry and endorse the joint purpose by humming or nodding.
- Data under investigation should be spoken aloud in the office, each Adjuster taking a paragraph in turn, interspersed with interpretation. In this way a compressed and layered history can begin to be formulated.

The Rogue and the Carniter
Part One

The Rogue Loss Adjuster travelled by stagecoach from London to Portland in a pair of heeled and ribboned shoes. His soles remained spotless. Portland was a familiar name to him as, following the Great Fire, many of London's prominent buildings had been reconstructed using quarried stone taken from its ground. The buildings and their stone edifices were impressive, but for the Rogue the prospect of this visit to their source was underwhelming. The journey itself was an incommodious chore and, once deposited on the southern shoreline of Weymouth, he was alarmed to find himself with no acceptable means of being carried across the sea. He had heard that Portland was not a true island, however at that time it was only joined to the mainland by way of Chesil: a narrow and practically impassable bank of loose shingle. And, perhaps the ferry had been overcome by rough waters, because the Rogue braved a sea crossing to the island on nothing more than a small fisherman's boat. Ropes guided the humble vessel during its volatile journey. Those gnarled and weathered strands offered little reassurance. Though the distance across was in fact relatively short, the Rogue would recount it as a voyage that took a full half hour, all the while tormented by waves and seagulls. He endured this ordeal with fingers clinging to the boat, securing his life as tenuously as the shingle tethered Portland to the mainland. When finally dropped ashore, he was sick stomached and dishevelled, his fine shoes soaked through.

The Rogue rested in the Portland Arms in the village of Fortuneswell. Ostensibly, he was there to investigate a possible need for Loss Adjustment on Portland further to the recent upsurge in the volume of quarrying. Taking no interest in stone and judging the assignment to be insignificant, he sat moodily in the corner of the saloon bar where he was asked if he desired a supper. Having suffered such a dreadful journey to reach the parochial limitations of this small isle, his expectations of an enjoyable meal were low. His stomach still to recover, he'd declined both breakfast and luncheon and was fully prepared to turn his nose away from dinner when a man approached him. In a local accent he introduced himself as Bartie Comben. Comben recommended the pork or the mutton, and he would know, for he was Carniter of the Court Leet.

On the journey down the Rogue Adjuster had heard about the Court Leet. Not such a rare institution at the time, it was the local authority that acted like a franchise of the Crown's criminal jurisdiction. The Court Leet's members had roles, including the Hayward, responsible for the common land, the Bailiff who administered arrests and summonses and supervised the removal of stone, and the Bread Weigler, who ensured the quality of the bread. Carniter was Bartie Comben's position; he assessed local meat and poultry, and as such could be trusted to attest to the good quality of a cut of mutton, or of a pork chop.

The Rogue momentarily considered that he might fancy the Carniter's food-eating role for himself. Such work would suit him well, he thought, and he could doubtless perform any duties with greater flair than the man standing in front of him. Starting to dribble, he leaned forward as if about to bite but instead announced that he refused to eat pig. They were filthy creatures who would happily consume human flesh. He sat back after saying this, as if to judge the Carniter's response, and then, on hearing a rumble of hunger emerge from beneath his waistcoat, said he could, however, be convinced of a sheep. He was informed that there at the Portland Arms he could dine on the finest local mutton. In recent months it had been approved by no less than the monarch, who when holidaying in Weymouth, came across to Portland, stayed at this very inn, and consumed a bowl of mutton stew with notable enthusiasm. The dinner was sold. But the Carniter, Bartie Comben, would not let the Rogue pay for the meal; the cost would be more than made up by the satisfaction of seeing such a respectable visitor enjoy the local fayre. In this way persuaded, the Rogue devoured a roasted shank of Portland mutton.

As he chewed through the softened sinews of the dead creature's leg, he wondered at Bartie Comben's generosity and recalled being told that the Court Leet roles were agreed to, not for any significant financial reward, but as an honour, and as such were generally undertaken with due respect for the position and the island's traditions. The Rogue's suspicion that this meal would be paid for in one way or another rendered unto the otherwise sweet meat a tinge of bitterness.

By the time the Rogue was back in London he had decided on a plan of action. He invited the Carniter, Bartie Comben, to Lloyd's Coffee House.

On his first trip to the City, the Carniter, ill at ease, discovered he had no taste for coffee, spitting the liquid back into the saucer after every mouthful. The Rogue pounced, immediately announcing that he required a quarterly assignment of live Portland sheep and that it was within Comben's gift to supply it. Among the more discerning rich, there was a market for uncommon delicacies and a slice of the profits would be passed on to Comben.

The Carniter, Bartie Comben, stated that he would, for the time being, send the sheep to London by ship, along with the stone, but that the Rogue and his customers should be aware that these sheep required the common land of Portland to graze on. It would be the case, he added, that if the furious pace of quarrying of the island's stone was maintained, there would be, by his estimation, within the next one hundred years, nowhere for the sheep to graze. What was then known as Portland would, in time, be nothing but a pillaged wasteland. He said that he believed that the right thing for the Rogue to do, would be to use these sheep as a way to convince his clients that Portland was worth more than its stone, and if they indeed wanted to enjoy the delights of its mutton, the place needed to remain a viable grazing land.

The Rogue told the Carniter that he couldn't manage such a radical redirection of interest on the basis of the occasional roast dinner. His slobbery tongue passed around his lips between sentences. Besides, he said, the less land there was, the rarer the sheep, the more valuable they would be as a commodity.

Bartie Comben, the Court Leet Carniter, got to his feet. London had been rebuilt and was now impressive because of Portland, he said, but there were now great holes left in the island from which such structures were wrenched — this could not continue. He hit the table. The saucer wobbled, so displacing its umber contents onto the white tablecloth. Could the Rogue not see that London had been repaired only at the cost of destroying another part of England? The Carniter said that Portland, the sheep's grazing land, and nothing less than his own authority, was in danger of disappearing under his boots.

The Rogue looked down at the Carniter's boots and convulsed with laughter. 'You're in need of my money, Comben, both you and your decrepit island.' Mimicking the Carniter, he spat his own coffee onto the stained tablecloth in front of him then dabbed at his tears of mirth with the richly embroidered handkerchief that he extracted from his pocket. Still chuckling, he shook the handkerchief out with affected flamboyance, then held it across his face, as if to suppress his snorts, while every so often he peered over the top of it, to study the Portlander.

After he walked away from the Coffee House, Bartie Comben stopped in the shadow of an altitudinous Doric column of Portland stone named as the Monument to the

Great Fire of London. He'd heard that this shaft contained a miraculous device, a telescope to view the zenith of distant celestial spheres as they passed overhead. He didn't dare to look up. Instead, he put his hand on one of the blocks at the Monument's base and fingered the tiny cast of a Jurassic mollusc. Then he walked the short distance along Cannon Street until he reached St Paul's Cathedral. He slowed as he approached. Tears spilt from the belittled Carniter's eyes as he squinted, trying to absorb the scale of his small island's displacement.

- After presenting the first part of the story, disperse for a short break. During this free time, without the reassurance of each other's company, appear disorientated: drift gloomily in and out of musty alcoves, shuffle across worn carpet and into the various dim corners of the office. When these circumstances become intolerable, reconvene to recall the next part of the story.
- On realising that the narrative is incomplete, advance from agitation to excitement before reverting to standard despondency. Engage with the fragment. Beware of filling in the gaps, enquire instead into the discontinuity of the writing, as a process of adjustment.

The Rogue and the Carniter
Part Two

Given the pressing need for a vast man-made harbour off the Weymouth coast, a coincidence was contrived to combine this social necessity with Portland's limestone treasure and a renewable supply of unwaged workers in the form of prisoners brought there to do hard labour. The result was a spectacular industrial operation. The breakwater works balanced the dislocation of male felons from the mainland with the displacement of Portland's mass. Subversive criminality was exchanged for beneficial subservience; brutish destruction transformed into productive energy. The strength drawn from men who were emasculated by their loss of freedom, emerged reconditioned and modified in the form of noble civic constructions.

The Adjusters note the equation of the removal of stone from Portland with the intake of prisoners. Over the years, many men have been brought here and incarcerated at the Verne Citadel, or at the Young Offenders Institution in HM Prison, Portland and even on the Weare prison ship. Having been dislocated from their homes, these convicts have quarried stone and sent it back to the mainland, and in this way the prisoners have counterbalanced their presence on the island. In the present day, although the intake of convicts persists, and stone continues to be removed by free quarrymen, it is of concern that the simple neutralising displacement of the former arrangement, the correlation of human mass that was transported to Portland with the stone that they themselves then sent away from its shores, no longer occurs. An inability to account for the presence of these men is noted to be potentially unsettling. A prisoner might decide to remain on Portland indefinitely, for example. In which case all hope of calculating equilibrium in the balance of deficits and surpluses would be lost.

Built entirely of Portland stone, the harbour is composed of more than two miles of breakwater walls, drawn out across the sea in sweeping arcs. No less than three forts were erected on the breakwater, the largest of which stood some mile and a half from land. In order to get to the stone the convicts had first to build the road that led to the quarries. They had also constructed a church for themselves, as well as their own prison and their own stone cells inside it. They dug their own resting places in more ways than one, as by this time convict deaths at Portland were at the rate of one man per week.

A multifaceted amphitheatre was formed from this peculiar set of institutional and geological conditions at the convict quarries. The stage was of broken ground and deep crevices with natural walls that appeared more strikingly white the further they were from the earth's surface. Convicts laboured in these deep cavities driven on by prison wardens. Great blocks of stone from these depressions were lifted in cranes by the felons, and swung on to carriages, then dragged away along tramways. Mounds of rubble were piled on all sides. The first tier of a viewing area was formed by these raised areas. On them stood armed sentries in lookout stations. Opposite them, the higher viewing level was more varied; composed of numerous guest houses and taverns that had been established to cater to the tastes of the tourists who paid to enjoy the spectacle of convicts at work in the quarries. It was here that two men in paid employment planned to meet; one of them looking to swindle a few additional pounds on the side. They were the Rogue Adjuster's progeny, himself a Rogue Adjuster, and the incumbent Court Leet Carniter, again a Bartie Comben.

The Adjusters note that between Part One and Part Two of the writer's story, there's a shift from the eighteenth to nineteenth century but a suggestion that the descendants of the characters are congruent. While it is acknowledged that the story is framed as a fiction, the question remains as to whether the Rogue they currently pursue could be in any way related to the historical figure in the narrative. It is beyond rationality to think that he could be a reincarnation of the original Rogue. Implausibly, he appears to have evolved into an inextinguishable life form. Augmenting the supplementary mental dossier, the Rogue is to be studied as an antithetical physical entity who might exist in the permanent beyond. Shifting between vanishing and full manifestation, his unorthodox appearances are seen as fleeting indicators of the inverted supersensible world.

These incidents on Portland are primarily of local significance, but should be seen in relation to the Loss Adjusters' aim to maintain a material equilibrium worldwide. The case will be referred to counterpart Adjusters in Switzerland. Although these colleagues are currently preoccupied with the search for physical extremes, as an enquiry tangential to investigations appertaining to antimatter, the Rogue's condition is likely to be of concern. Drawing on the laws of thermodynamics, and emphasised for their attention, is the hypothesis that the Rogue's total energy remains constant, maintaining his material presence, regardless of the implausibility of his everyday existence.

- Address further paragraphs from Part Two of the writing. Take it in turns to recount the story. Progress in rotation and nod, slowly amassing an agreement on the consideration of the passages that require deliberation:

The two men sat across the table from each other, wordlessly quaffing ale. From the adjacent, non-convict quarry, there came the pulsing songs and chants of Portland's indigenous free quarrymen, pursuing their work in the traditional manner. Co-ordinated sound resonated throughout the arena; the repeated impact of iron against rock. The power required for a human body to force a pickaxe through stone required this rhythm.

As he sat tapping his leather-clad foot, the Rogue's mind was running through the machinations of his deal with the Carniter. Retrieving a black silk ribbon from his pocket, the Rogue tied his long hair back from his face and grimaced, revealing two gleaming teeth amidst the general decay in his mouth. He informed the Carniter that during recent dentistry work, he had in fact turned down the offer of golden teeth in favour of this bespoke pair — could the Carniter identify out of what material they were fashioned? He didn't wait for a response but revealed that he'd had the teeth specially contrived from Portland stone.

This information drew the Carniter's attention to the Rogue's mouth from which drooling cavity there next emerged a complaint. In recent months the mutton he had received was of a markedly inconsistent quality; in particular it lacked the sweetness to which his tongue was accustomed. Comben's response was frank: he called the Rogue an ignorant pig of a man. He said the sheep were from elsewhere because, as long predicted, Portland's grazing land had all but disappeared. The ruination of the island was seemingly unstoppable. And the matter of his profit was yet to be addressed. To date Comben had seen only pennies.

The Rogue said that he would not accept sheep from elsewhere and monies would only be exchanged when the supply was consistent and guaranteed. He added that Comben was missing the point; the increasing rarity of the sheep would be advantageous for business and this was certainly not about his own desperation to capture the last few animals for himself.

The Adjusters note that the Writer-in-Residence's story depends on further illogicalities. The Rogue realises that an overlooked consequence of quarrying is the removal of grazing land for Portland's native sheep. In his degenerate mind, he understands that this delicacy will become rare, so he attempts to secure a supply of it for himself, to fulfil an improbable level of demand from some unspecified market. Paradoxically, he needs the land to continue to disappear in order for the sheep to become increasingly valuable, leading to the nonsensical storyline in which he desires the very thing that will ultimately destroy his business. Such is the contorted logic of the Rogue's dealings.

When Comben accused him of being caught in the escalating illogicality of his greed, the Rogue stood up and prepared to leave. He stated that if he had to overthrow Comben and become Court Leet Carniter himself to get his hands on Portland's sheep, then he would do so. He departed for the bridge to the mainland, already beginning to contrive his return.

The Adjusters note the Rogue's deviance from routine loss adjustment procedures. This is an outstanding offence: instead of counterbalancing Portland's losses by addressing them conceptually and physically, instead of manipulating the absence of stone and the displacement of objects as might a sculptor, the Rogue attempts to capitalise on these instabilities, and with conspicuous pleasure. In his crude and false accounting he suggests that it is possible to maintain both the sheep and the quarrying. The Adjusters are in agreement that they experience the narrative as a cautionary tale. Data will be compiled to appraise the exact nature of the shocking misdemeanors committed by this maverick member of the fraternity, who operates beyond their rules.

Bartie Comben sat for a while and attempted to calm himself by resting his hand on the rounded paunch of his gut. The only other people in the room with him at that time were a young woman and the proprietor of the guest house. The woman was seated, but leaning forward. Appalled but fascinated by the spectacle provided by the convict workmen, she repeatedly complained to the proprietor that the prisoners looked about to expire from the cruelty of their labour. As she spoke, she rubbed each of her fingers in turn, compulsively, giving the impression of some deeper anxiety. While he watched the woman across the room, Comben stroked the extended band of leather, with its scrotum-like sac, that hung from his belt. Finally he approached her and suggested that there were postcards available on the premises, for those who found the spectacle so compelling. She could, he said, select an image of a guard overseeing the convict labour at that very quarry. He picked one up from the end of the serving bar to show her. There was less to offend her on the mainland, she should head back there, he said. The woman snatched the postcard from the Carniter's hand. Ignoring his derision, she paid the proprietor but remained on the scene to study the card's dispassionate reproduction of her disturbing surroundings.

The Adjusters note that the woman in the story is unnamed. Filing back through collected metadata on the writer's material output it is estimated that this character could be the writer herself, making an appearance in the fiction. She is compelled to step in to attend to the inconsistencies of her incomplete chronicle, but once there, she becomes distracted by the volatile context. Finding there is no solid ground for the narrative, and no logical place for the story to go, she remains a helpless voyeur.

After he had tipped the last of his drink down his gullet, the Carniter left the tavern. He hurried along the torn-up eastern path, south until he reached Yeolands Quarry. There, outside of its working hours, he was at liberty to wander across its valuable resource. He stopped and caught his breath, releasing the sling from his waist as he did so. Then he bent down and sorted through some small stones on the ground with expert speed. If the finest Basebed stone had been available he would have rejected it along with the surface rubble. He sought the shelly Whitbed, with its sharp irregular edges. The selected object was placed into the sling and drawn back. He scanned and waited. He was prepared to wait for many years if that was what was required to rid the island of vermin. Up popped a rabbit, bounding across his sight. Calmly, he fired off a stone that hit the animal directly between its proud furry ears. The precise impact of the missile to the creature's unwitting brain killed it outright.

The Adjusters note that the investigation raises the negative possibilities of their professional condition and, judging the story to be incomplete, it is now crucial to discover an additional part. They will search through the writer's deleted files for an ending or Addendum. If, in the final analysis, this text is not uncovered, they can, at the very least, expect to be conscious of their own perceptions of that absence.

The Adjusters surmise that Portland is an astonishing zone of vanishing physicality. It demands to be counterbalanced with extreme sensual encounters and critical understandings, but given the Rogue's reckless mode of operating, such encounters might manifest in the form of physical violence. It is concluded that it is essential to remain on the island until the Rogue is unearthed. This compact ensures an indefinite period, during which time the broader enquiry into Portland stone can be pursued.

Addendum

Without exception, it is death that precedes the employment of our beardless youth. Here's Ash today, beyond his teenage years but young in relation to the planet and frantically labouring, hacking at its resistant surface. In his eyes there's a near tearful passion. A pickaxe repeatedly elevated in his hands is brought down to pierce, stab and jostle through stone. A spade to cut through, stamped in and levered, raises stone that's hurled aside.

When he started digging this hole by daylight, he had recourse to his pneumatic drill and the nifty mechanical digger that created the precisely rectangular six-foot ditch he's currently standing in. He thought the job was done but he has returned tonight, compelled to dig another two feet down, covertly. But now, with his physical labour alone he powers his pickaxe into the stone. The Carniter's corpse lies in a wheelbarrow at the graveside.

Before the Carniter's murder, Ash did time in the Young Offenders Institution at the Grove across on the east coast of the island. While inside he took a liking to the place he occasionally glimpsed. Seen through narrow windows, the island was, for him, a fractured and enchanting spectacle. When they let him out, this quality appeared heightened and instead of returning to his London home, he remained on Portland.

That spring, when he first left the Young Offenders Institution at HM Prison, Portland, the officers gave him the regular discharge grant, a stack of advice leaflets and emergency numbers. The only belongings he collected were the clothes he came in and a backpack. In it he found an old magazine about organized crime, a book on the life of mammals and two lead soldiers (one scrambling on his stomach holding his rifle up, over his head, and the other, down on one knee, taking aim). There was no-one to pick him up, but he didn't want to be seen in any case. Having grown broader, his clothes were embarrassingly small. In spite of being stretched until it covered his midriff, his sweater sprung back up to his navel. He zipped his jacket against the cool air and advanced in constrained paces, taking care not to test the seams of his trouser fabric. As he stepped through the gateway, the officers pointed him towards the mainland. Once there he could hop on a train back to London, they said.

He was soon outside the Clifton Hotel, just a few hundred yards from the prison. And seconds later he was inside and placing an order. He pushed his fingers into his taut pocket. The discharge grant was retrieved and imparted to the bartender. 'I want a pint of lager,' he said, then added, 'and a bottle of fizzy water and two packets of salt-and-vinegar crisps.' Less than ten minutes later he was back on the street. With the pint in his gut and the supplies in his sack, he stood and drew a deep breath. This air was the transmitter that had conveyed particles of the landscape into his cell. It smelled of the mineral mingling of sea salt and limestone and tasted like the source of life.

Instead of heading for the mainland, he went back the way he'd come, straight past the prison gate, where he took a sharp left, towards the sea. Through a gap in the low shrubs he found a fragmented footpath. He stood for a while and waited, looking seaward over the rocky landscape they call the East Weare. A wild goat moved on the cliff-edge in small but rapid steps. With fearless agility it skipped across the precarious stone. Ash called out, 'Hello.' He lingered, fascinated by the beast's dainty ability to negotiate his freedom, with sure footing on every risky plane and crevice. 'Cloven hooves step lightly over strange terrain,' he said.

He peered down at his own awkward feet, then crouched and picked a loose stone from the path. At the crutch of his trousers a small tear appeared. It was at the seam and not indecent. The irregular object in his hand was cut through with its own black seam. He tried to assess the form by counting its surfaces and discerning the multiple differentiations in its tone, but he was quickly defeated by the impossible complexity of its planes, angles and colours, ranging from oblique to obtuse, through shadow and bright reflected white. 'Smoky flint,' he said aloud. 'Grey, matt cream, little spots of silver, beige and lime. I'd bet there's not one other stone exactly like this one anywhere else in the whole world.'

He turned to face the high prison wall built from the same land, topped off with electrified fencing and coils of barbed wire. He lobbed his stone over it. Then he picked up others and threw a volley over the wall, at which point the alarms went off and he scrambled into the scrub until he was well away from the place. He headed south down narrow steps that led onto the old railway trackbed at the lowest level of the coastal path.

So far as he could tell no one was attempting to pursue him; still, the young man hurried, keeping his head down below the tops of bushes. He passed enormous slabs of rock abandoned in mounds and small scatterings. At one time these stones had been swung out on derricks towards waiting vessels below, while others, discarded as waste, were rolled off the cliffs. He had the impression of the island falling away at its edges.

The wild goat, with its cloven hooves, stood on a high and narrow vantage point and watched.

When Ash reached the promontory, beside the remains of Rufus Castle, he could see an array of huts below him at Church Ope Cove. He climbed down then stopped and took cover in the bushes. The huts were all wooden, the size of small sheds. He thought they must have contained only a single room. Garden-like areas were demarcated by low walls built of large, smoothed stones taken from the Cove itself. It looked like a primeval village, established by an archaic tribe who had come ashore here. He decided the sheds were likely to be holiday cabins. It was not high season, yet, but still he monitored the area to make sure there was no one about.

Opting for a small hut away from the footpath, he approached cautiously, picking up a heavy rock from the beach as he drew nearer. He pounded on the door's padlock until it sprung open, and he was in. The room was furnished with a narrow bunk and a chair, not unlike those in his cell. There was a window, but the view of the sea was blocked by planks, perhaps in an attempt to make it secure. It was moving towards evening, but there was still a little light inside by virtue of a small opening between the boards on the side of the hut that faced inland. Ash took one of the packets of crisps from his backpack, tore it open and started eating. His rapid crunching slowed as he detected warmth about the place. Dropping the crisps on the floor, he took flight up the hillside and into a wooded grove.

Among the trees, a group of stone ruins and tumbledown graves provided an obscure recess; a place to sleep that promised an uncomfortable night. Just a couple of hours later he opened his eyes. There was a tarpaulin over his body. It must have been nearby and somehow, in the night, it had settled on him, 'Blown by the wind,' he said out loud, then he returned to sleep. In the middle of the night he was woken again. Someone had lifted the tarpaulin and had crept in under it. The shock should have made him hit out, but his nerves were settled by a woman's 'shhh' with the reassurance of her fingers on his mouth and her skin warmer than his own. Strangely, she slipped her hand through the hole at the seam of his trousers. She wanted to kiss him. She kissed him then struggled to take his trousers off. He might have helped her to do this. When she finally left, she robbed him of his remaining packet of crisps. At dawn, roused by his mouth watering, Ash gave up on further sleep. At his side he found a small silver package. Hot to the touch and wrapped in foil, it was an entire roasted creature, possibly a rabbit.

The following night he stayed awake, vigilant. No one passed by, and there was no surprise provision of sex or of food when either would have done. The next morning he decided to move on.

When he came up from the Cove, and into the villages, the people he initially encountered were Portlanders, with no inclination to violence. As the weeks went by he got cash-in-hand work here and there but he continued to sleep rough. There was no shortage of food: he rummaged in the bins at Tesco for out-of-date sandwiches and found sufficient to leave some for the goat back out on the East Weare. Although it never fed from his hand, they had established a degree of trust, he felt. Soon he'd saved enough to rent a room at the top of a small house in Weston, adjacent to Bowers Quarry and the municipal cemetery where he eventually found his current job. From the window of his bedroom he enjoyed looking across this landscape, but the best view was from the edge of the quarry itself. He imagined seeing dinosaurs. There were cavities so deep that they revealed whole periods of time compacted in layers of stone going right back to the Jurassic age. It made him think that part of his job was to dig into the past. If he turned at one particular spot he saw the prison over on the horizon, then the church built out of the same stone, as were the graves and tombs he could see in the old cemetery and the holes he was employed to dig in the new one.

Until today Ash has fulfilled the duties of his employment efficiently. He has acquired the necessary skills to maintain the grounds and to conceal bodies under stony rubble, legitimately. People have trusted him with their deaths. All except the Carniter have been right to do so: his burial a misdemeanour and his ending, a murder, too abrupt.

Postscript

The Municipal Cemetery, Weston — Night
Ash is frantically labouring, digging up the ground, turning stones. His pickaxe goes in, sending tiny particles of hard flint flying up towards his face, splinters of an archaeological order unsettled, threatening to blind him. Exhausted and shaking he clambers out of the grave. The dead Carniter lies in a wheelbarrow by his side.

> **Ash**
> [inner thoughts]
> This must be deep enough.

He moves the wheelbarrow to the edge of the cavity, grips the handles and hauls them up. The Carniter's big-gutted corpse tips out of the tray and tumbles heavily into the hole. Working fast, Ash shovels stony rubble over the body then pulls the steel lid over the top of the grave.

> **Ash**
> [inner thoughts]
> It's done. And tomorrow, there'll be a coffin on top of the rubble. And then the hole will be filled to the ground.

He slumps at the graveside. There's a large mound of earth next to him: the displaced overburden that will no longer fit back into the cavity. An ad hoc arrangement of vertical boards, propped up with rusty iron rods prevents this mass from spreading. Ash sits back and stares at the mound formed by the surplus of freshly dug rubble. He tries to look past and around it.

Ash
[inner thoughts]
But I thought I was hiding the corpse. I don't understand. I've made an incriminating pile of stone … It's almost the same size as the Carniter's body. It is the Carniter's body, debased! I've got to get rid of it.

He grabs the spade quickly, shovelling and loading the wheelbarrow. Just as soon as it's loaded he pushes the barrow out of Weston. He heads across Wide Street then negotiates an uneven and narrow track behind the cricket pitch. He crosses the next main street at Easton and wheels along to the very end of Grove Road. On passing the prison he averts his eyes.

Ash
[inner thoughts]
Can't stop now … Keep moving … Don't look back.

The East Weare, the Grove — Dawn
Behind the prison, Ash leaves the barrow by the roadside and steps through bushes and onto the coast path. There's a goat on the cliff-edge, looking out to sea. Taking a seat on the rock, he calls up to it.

Ash
Hey, something really bad happened to me today. I'll tell you but you've got to keep this one to yourself, okay?

The Goat
[silence]

Ash
I'm serious. I'm not making this up … I was standing inside an official grave. I heard footsteps and singing above, on Weston Road. I looked over the edge of the grave really carefully. I saw five men. By the sound of them, they'd just stepped out of The George. They were singing what might have been quarrymen's songs. They all looked like they were getting on a bit but they were well built, like they'd been trained in the old ways. You know, people who'd moved the land with their hands and a pickaxe. And there can't be many of them left now. But they were almost out of sight when one of them turned and lifted his cap, nodding his head towards me, just slightly, like he was greeting a comrade or something like that. By the time I waved back at the old man, he'd turned and was gone. At that moment a small black object blew past my hand and the wind dropped it into the grave. It was a strip of ribbon and it landed right next to my feet at the bottom of the hole. But before I could pick it up I heard another noise. There were two men not far behind the quarrymen. They were arguing. Well they didn't expect anyone underground to be alive and listening, did they? One of them was saying he'd done his research … he knew the sheep were back, he wanted his meat … he expected to get what he wanted. The other man was calmer. He said, Yes, that's right … the Portland breed had returned to the island, and it was true that they were out on Fancy's Farm, but there was a problem …

there was only a single healthy flock on the island … any significant trade in them wasn't sustainable. A passing car stopped me from hearing what was said next, but the tone of the conversation got more aggressive. By the time the car had gone, the two men were out of earshot. I saw them as they walked out of the cemetery gate. Even from that far, I recognised the potbellied one as a local — Bartie Comben, the Court Leet Carniter. I'd seen that Carniter there before, killing rabbits in the quarry with his slingshot, but the man with him, he was an outsider. I'd have recognised him if he lived on Portland. With that shoulder-length hair, he looked a bit seedy, like a rogue. And then they were gone.

The goat turns its head in Ash's direction, briefly sniffing the air as if for any sign of food before returning to his investigation of the small shrubs growing between the stones on the cliff-edge.

Ash

I'll bring you food next time, okay? It's been difficult today. Where was I? … I took my usual route out of the cemetery, through the old graveyard at St George's. I stepped really carefully over tombs and out from the north gate, took a sharp left on the public footpath then left again along the scrubland on the outside edge of the graveyard wall. So I had Bowers quarry ahead of me — a sheer drop. You should go there sometime. You could make your way there, sure you could. Or I could take you there in my barrow if you like. You'd love it … What's that?

There's a low sound like the soft murmur of voices, coming from just behind Ash. He jumps to his feet. The noise stops. There are shrubs and rocks and among them various tiny creatures creating small disturbances.

Ash
Did you hear something?

The goat makes no indication of having heard anything.

Ash
Anyway, as I was saying, I was in the quarry and I saw the Carniter with his slingshot, I thought he was shooting rabbits but then, running between the stones, less than five metres from where I was hiding, I saw not a rabbit, but him, that long-haired Rogue. A moment later he fell, downed by a stone fired off by the Carniter. I ducked behind a boulder, keeping low, like this. He got him first time, but when the Carniter ran over for a closer look, the Rogue was on his feet. They wrestled and the Rogue snatched the weapon then wrapped it around the Carniter's throat and pulled it tighter and tighter. He throttled him with his own sling. The Carniter fell to the ground, dead. Seconds later, and with his hair blowing behind him, that Rogue ran past, out of Bowers and across Wide Street down into that network of paths in Inmosthay. I jumped up and followed. I'm as nimble as you now. Nimble and undetectable. There's no way he could get the better of me. No fucking way. The wind picked up, so although the rubble was really crunchy, I could stay close enough to tail him, without being heard. I got to the high

ground and watched. I was lucky there was a big moon. And there he was, bleeding from the head and moving really awkwardly. I could have taken him on if I'd wanted. If I had horns like yours, I'd have run him through. I know those tracks. Most of them go around Inmosthay and cut across Jordans working quarry, or they just kind of fade away into the wasteland … I know what you're thinking … where was he going, right? Really, you'd have thought he was a complete idiot if you'd seen the way he walked. He must have had some really stupid shoes on. I thought he might head through the tunnel at Tout but he came out near the electrical shop on Easton Road, then he kept going past the Heights up New Ground towards the High Angle Battery. I took the shortcut across the open field and got there just before him. Even through the wind I could hear him trotting around in his fancy heeled shoes. What a wanker. I called out to him like this, 'Where d'ya think you're going?' But there's a powerful echo in those old magazine tunnels so it sounded really loud. He turned around. He put his hand to his head and started swaying, like he was giddy from his wound, but he did this weirdo smile with bright white teeth. He wanted to know who I was. I told him I saw him do that killing. He said no one would believe me. He said, I was there, so he'd blame the murder on me. My word against his.

The goat, who had been browsing for the duration of this monologue, now takes up a semi-reclining position, lowering its body to the ground, tucking three legs under its chest, leaving one at the front outstretched.

Ash sits on his haunches. This allows him to bounce a little, in this way animating his narrative.

Ash

That Rogue said the Carniter was dead and that he, the Rogue, would now be the new Carniter of the Court Leet! He said he'd get away with the murder and the sheep, that he'd eat mutton until he burst. He wasn't walking straight. I could've taken him on. I reckon he must've lost loads of blood. Then he ran up the steps and across the road towards Fancy's Farm. He climbed the fence and tumbled through the barbed wire. That must've hurt and I mean, what did he do that for? When he got to the other side he just ran towards one of the pens, turned a bucket over and scrambled up that chain-linked fence to get into the enclosure. I stayed outside the Farm. If I went in and grabbed his legs, I could have taken him down with one move and then I'd have had him and I could have fucked him up or whatever. But then the snorting started. It was the pig's pen. He was stuck halfway over. His trouser leg was caught on the wires. 'That's right, you hang upside down, you stupid fucking idiot,' I said. He didn't even have the strength to swing his body up and get himself out of there. I saw his trousers ripping. I was still outside the perimeter fence but I saw everything. He fell head-first, straight onto the stone at the edge of the sty. It was brutal. I mean, the cracking of his skull was really loud. I stepped back from the fence, then forward. I gripped the wire. I knew that pigs eat almost anything that's put in front of them; they'd eat a fallen man left unconscious in their enclosure. They were already on the way to their trough, snuffling and snorting. A light flashed on in one of the farm buildings. I just sort of recoiled. What would you have done? I wish you'd say something. Maybe it's good that you're quiet ... You're right, fuck it, I was more concerned with my own safety than the man I'd just seen murder the Carniter. A torch beam scanned across the farm and I dived to the ground, in the shadow of the old guardhouse. Then the lights went off and the pigs got to work. Nasty business ... What could I do? I slowly traced my path back, all the way across Inmosthay. I was thinking on the way, those owners of Fancy's Farm, they'd never know what happened to the Rogue. The wind would take his long strands of hair away from the scene. Pigs can't digest teeth either, but they'd be camouflaged against the land. In the right circumstances, it's an undetectable death ... I wondered about those sheep he was after. They must have been still sleeping in their enclosure on the other side of the farm. It's only the ordinary sheep that are kept outside, the special Portland ones are protected, hidden in a shed. He didn't even see them. By the time I got back to Bowers I thought I'd imagined everything, until I reached the spot where I last saw the real Carniter. I wanted to walk around the stone and find nothing, but his body was still there. I thought of the emergency helpline numbers I'd been given when they let me out of the prison, I thought of the bottom of holes that I couldn't climb out of, I thought of your cloven hoof. If I'd had a cloven hoof I could get out of any situation, but I haven't got one and the Rogue said that I'll be blamed for Bartie Comben's death ... Did you say something?

The goat looks like it's sleeping.

Behind Ash, a few leaves in the bushes rustle with movement. He looks around before proceeding more quietly.

Ash
I ran to my workshed and came back with my wheelbarrow, heaved the Carniter into the tray and off I went, wheeling through the gaps between the stones, out of the quarry and back across the cemetery until I reached a fresh grave I'd been digging for someone else. I dug deeper then tipped him in the hole but I can't seem to get rid of him … Did you hear that? Who is it?

Ash pauses. From the shrubs, just behind where he's sitting, two men and a woman emerge.

The Loss Adjusters
We're the Loss Adjusters from Easton.

Ash stands up, as if to attention.

Loss Adjuster No. 1
We saw you crossing the road very close to our offices. Intrigued by the unaccounted-for mass that you conveyed in your wheelbarrow, we resolved to follow you. We stood here and listened to your story. Your claim to have seen the end of the Rogue leaves us with a series of well-founded suspicions.

Loss Adjuster No. 2
Yes, suspicions, heightened by the convenient indiscernibility of evidence. Let's say that your chronicle requires some fine-tuning as we generally expect to counterbalance loss with a presence.

Loss Adjuster No. 3
The issues this case raises are complicated by your multifarious assets and liabilities.

Loss Adjuster No. 1
And his tendency to fantasise.

Loss Adjuster No. 2
And your tendency to fantasise, as alluded to throughout your narrative.

The Loss Adjusters all nod in agreement. They then turn away from Ash to instead convene in a consolidated huddle.

The Loss Adjusters
When we next assemble with our fellow Adjusters, a new enquiry will be opened. The displacement of Portland stone is at the centre of this story. Yes, the material in this barrow is highly volatile, and when seen in relationship to the mortality it represents the potential consequences of its continuing dislocation are fascinating. He's in the process of relocating the rubble but there is nowhere for it to go. Its space has been filled. We are all in agreement. Yes. His burden is a loose memorial to the Carniter and ours is a doleful deduction. We must advise the young man to

push the stone for many years and possibly to continue to do so until the very end of his days.

The Goat

[inner thoughts]

Irregular ground under your feet, young man. You veer from side to side, unsteady. Step lightly. Keep moving … Come back with food.

Appendix (c)

Ostensible Format of Loss Adjusters' Report No. _
Retrieved From The Memory Archive
Further to The Loss of *The Writer-In-Residence*

Details of Displacement
Predicaments
Circumstances
Evidence of the Vanishing Present, etc.

Exhibits
Exhibit b) The writer-in-residence's computer.

There are a number of stories deleted by the writer and recovered by the Adjusters. The only text saved on the desktop is a proposal:

> *I will compose a text solely comprised of end matter such as an epilogue, a postscript, an afterword, some addenda, or appendices, etc. The shadowy quality of the work's documentary vestiges will act as a memento to the missing body of the book. It will be a form clearly appropriate for the supposedly absent meta-narrative.*

Exhibit c) audio file 2 of 2
Discovered on the writer's voice recorder.

Transcript of audio file:

'I'm a woman of advanced years, but not yet in the permanent beyond. I'm here in my flat above the Loss Adjusters' office at No. 52 Easton Street. I'm writing. I should be writing, but I want to go out. I'm going out. I'll have to go down the stairs and through the door that leads me to their office. There's no other way out to the street. As usual I can't hear anything from down there. I never hear any sound from below. It's as if I reside above a void. Once I thought I heard their front door swing shut. I remember dashing to my bay window. There was a group of men and women walking northwards up the street. Perhaps they were heading towards the Cove House Inn. They'd get a good pint there. They could have been my Adjusters, but equally they could have been passing locals. It's impossible to discern sufficient detail from such spectral figures in the twilight.

[PAUSE]
'When I go downstairs, I have to walk through their offices, but even then I never see anyone. There are no files or documents on their desks or in drawers. The cabinets are empty. It's an uninhabited space and invariably unsettling to walk through. I want to go out. There should be another way. Here, upstairs, I have to face this other uninhabited space — the empty document on my computer screen. I'm playing with my fingers again. I must stop this.

[FOOTSTEPS]
'I stood up and now I'm backing away from the laptop. I'm returning to my desk, sitting down then getting up

and backing away again. I need to get back to my desk. I need to get away. This is exhausting. I'm pulling my coat on and making my way, step by step, down the stairs. I should remember, this writing position on Portland is self-appointed, and, given my age, it's probably my final stab at producing a substantial volume of text. I admit that in many ways the text is in its early stages. It's time to leave but it's getting more difficult to go out and face the stones on the island. Their presence, and the manner in which they surface, are sitting ever more uncomfortably in my thoughts. It reminds me of all my past mistakes, all the writing I've tried to discard. Just the thought of it produces tension in my stomach. If it wasn't for the stone I could have had my book finished many months ago. Sometimes I believe the stones are inside me making it impossible to think of anything else. I recognise them as a *Stumbling Block* of course, and a build up of frustration and anger at the sheer impossibility of the subject. Or that might be the gallstones. They're inside my body, formed of a greenish-yellow and bitter-tasting acid and cholesterol-based fluid. This concentrated bile is the sort of matter that penetrates rather than passes through a body. I've googled the symptoms — abdominal pain, cramping: it seems likely. I've also heard the rumours about radon, that it's prevalent in this area and has been detected in the office. Maybe I'm being slowly poisoned by radon gas, that's perhaps absorbed from the office when I pass through it.

[RUSTLING]
'I've grabbed my bag and I'm heading down the stairs, as quickly as these stiff legs will allow. Why have I

stopped again? In order to reach the street I'll need to pass through the offices. There is no other way out. I'm closing the door. Now I'm walking slowly, back up the stairs into the flat. That's it. I've dropped my bag on the kitchen floor. Last week I managed to get out. At one time I went out nearly every day. I went to Bowers and I saw the corpse. I will have to leave at some point. But for now I'm getting back to work. I'm writing. I'm trying to write. I'm working on my manuscript.

[LONG PAUSE]
'I've not got very far with the writing. I know the text will be composed under chapter titles that suggest a book solely comprised of end matter, in other words there could be an epilogue, postscript, appendix, addendum etc. The plan is for the shadowy quality of the work's documentary vestiges to act as a memento to the missing body of the book. The form being appropriate for the supposedly absent meta-narrative. When I initially developed this idea it seemed conceptually neat and therefore easy to follow through. In practice I came here from London, rented this flat to write in, but have since produced little more than a few stories that I've deleted, and I wonder if the entire scheme isn't an end in itself. Something that's complete as a proposal. It also occurs to me that end matter is most usually associated with non-fiction, so I can't even make it up. But I'm increasingly convinced that the subject of the missing body matter should be missing, in the sense that it is nothing. Or more precisely, the body matter should be missing and if it is nothing and the end matter is the book, then the book is nothing.

I'm standing up again and I'm backing away from the laptop. Perhaps I could have made this work when I was younger. Perhaps it's a job for a younger woman. I try to write, but I'm going round in circles, repeating the same mistakes instead of moving forward. I admit that in many ways the writing is in its early stages, but I have to get out.

[FOOTSTEPS]
'I know I have to go back to Bowers Quarry. It's there that I can think through the text's conditions of possibility. I can just about walk there. My feet are tired and my stomach and shoulders are so strained but it's a different sort of pressure to that in my head.

[PAUSE]
'Sometimes it's hard to go out and face the holes in the island. The way the land's unsettled sits uncomfortably in my thoughts and produces tension in my stomach every time I attempt to write. If it wasn't for the holes I could have had my story finished many months ago. Paradoxically, the removal of stone only seems to create a greater and more complex surface area of yet more stone. There's an excess of it everywhere. I'm ready to go. I'm going. I'm passing through the spaces of the front office. Here's the unoccupied desk and the empty coat hooks. There's their blank pin board.

[FOOTSTEPS]
'I've stopped. I'm pressing each of my fingers in turn while I'm waiting. In order to reach the street I'll need to

pass through the offices. There is no other way out to the street. I'm closing the door and walking back up the stairs into the flat. Last week I managed to get out. I've got to break the cycle. At one time I went out nearly every day. I will have to leave at some point. But for now I'm getting back to work. I'm writing. I'm trying to write. I'm working on the manuscript. I'm standing up again. I've picked up my bag and now I'm slipping my right arm and my head into a loop formed by the leather strap. The strap has fallen across my chest allowing the handbag to rest on my thigh. This is it. I'm going to walk across the space, open the door and head out. I'm always inland, best to see some of the periphery of the island instead. I'll leave the recorder here and I'll take a proper walk around the coast. I might actually enjoy the precariousness of the ground underfoot. I'll start at the end of Chesil, by the huts on the West Weare.'

Postface

At Church Ope Cove, Miss Hazeline Horrocks is peering through the gap in her cabin wall, and into the shrubs, through which she sees Portland. She says, 'I saw the hut crushed and imagined the gruesome traces of a corpse turning on the surface of the stone. The body must have been so appallingly pressed in and pulverised, that it was unidentifiable. I just sort of collapsed and fell unconscious, on to the ground. Then someone lifted me. I was lifted to my feet. It was you, Celestine. You were with me.'

Celestine is holding her sister's hand as she speaks. 'That evening I took the No. 1 bus to Easton shopping centre, hoping to get there before closing. I was too late, so I planned to walk back along the road to my hut. I wandered up Reforne but just as I passed the cemetery I saw a young man struggling. He was pushing a wheelbarrow overloaded with rubble. He looked so distracted and beleaguered. Of course I wanted to help, I tried to stop him but when our paths crossed in the middle of Wide Street, he didn't even see me.'

'You got him didn't you?'

'No. He was in another world and it was a cold tormented place where I couldn't reach him. I felt a terrible sadness as we passed, something similar to a feeling of loss but with less reason than loss because it's for something I've never had, more like an unrequited love. Then he was gone and I was still in the middle of Wide Street in front of the graveyard.

Left unsure of which one of us wasn't really there, I shuddered. Before I walked back along Wide Street I had to stop at the George Inn for a cider and black. I might have had two. Well, it's a good thing I did, because I'm here now, aren't I Hazy.' She grips her sister's hand more tightly. 'I am here. I'm not dead. And it feels just right for us to live together, in a shared hut, here at Church Ope Cove.'

For a moment Hazeline turns to look at her sister's face, 'Whoever was killed that day was really very unlucky to be walking past at that calamitous moment.'

'Yeah, that person must have tried very hard to find such an unfortunate combination of circumstances.'

'Really, it was as if they pursued their own death,' says Hazeline. She repositions herself to gaze once again at Portland. 'The stone crushed the hut first and then rolled on to whoever was on the other side of it. When the emergency services came, they tried to turn the stone, but in doing so they set it off again. It rolled away from them and into the sea. If there were any remains, they couldn't be retrieved. They cleared away your old hut. It's long gone.'

Celestine nods. 'There's nothing to see.'

Appendix (d)

Ostensible Format of Loss Adjusters' Extraordinary Meeting Agenda No. _
Retrieved From The Memory Archive

1.1
We have recovered the stories from the writer's deleted folder. These are a collection of narratives about characters situated on Portland, including her shocking account of the Rogue Loss Adjuster and the story featuring the sisters named Horrocks, etc. In addition to our regular monitoring of fictive phenomena, our discussion should consider the possibility that some, or all, of these characters, might persist in the inverted *supersensible* world of the permanent beyond.

1.2
Some of the writer's stories suggest that she may have even speculated on, or been witness to, our own activities. During the meeting, these narratives will be addressed. Further to this, we will gauge how dependent we are on their existence. We will consider retaining the rejected texts.

1.3
We should continue to assess the negative qualities of Portland stone as the unstable ground on which events unfold. In addition, the difficulties of sustaining the reality of a disappearing object will be referred to. Our dossier on the way in which Portland is formed, through the layered compression of the past and the systematic displacement of its present,

will be useful in this respect. We note that this surfacing of the past might lead to increased incidence of formal dissonance.

1.4
The attempt to delete files, her preoccupation with a body, and the desire to forfeit the central mass of writing, in pursuit of an impossible text, will be examined as evidence that our writer-in-residence was cultivating loss.

1.5
The Loss Adjusters surmise that it would not be possible to successfully produce a book that is simultaneously *complete* and *nothing but* authentic end matter. What will the end matter refer to? If it refers to a second book, then the original book will not be complete. If the referred-to text is absent, then the addendum, postscript, etc., will in fact not be end matter at all, but will be body matter, masquerading as end matter. If the pages referred to by the postface, appendices, etc., are in the book but blank, they will suggest an erasure: but the content can not have been erased, as it has never been written. The book will need both text and end matter in place, meaning the project is unresolved and unresolvable. If such a text ever claims to exist it will be erroneously titled, or inauthentic, leaving the frustrated writer with no option but to disappear.

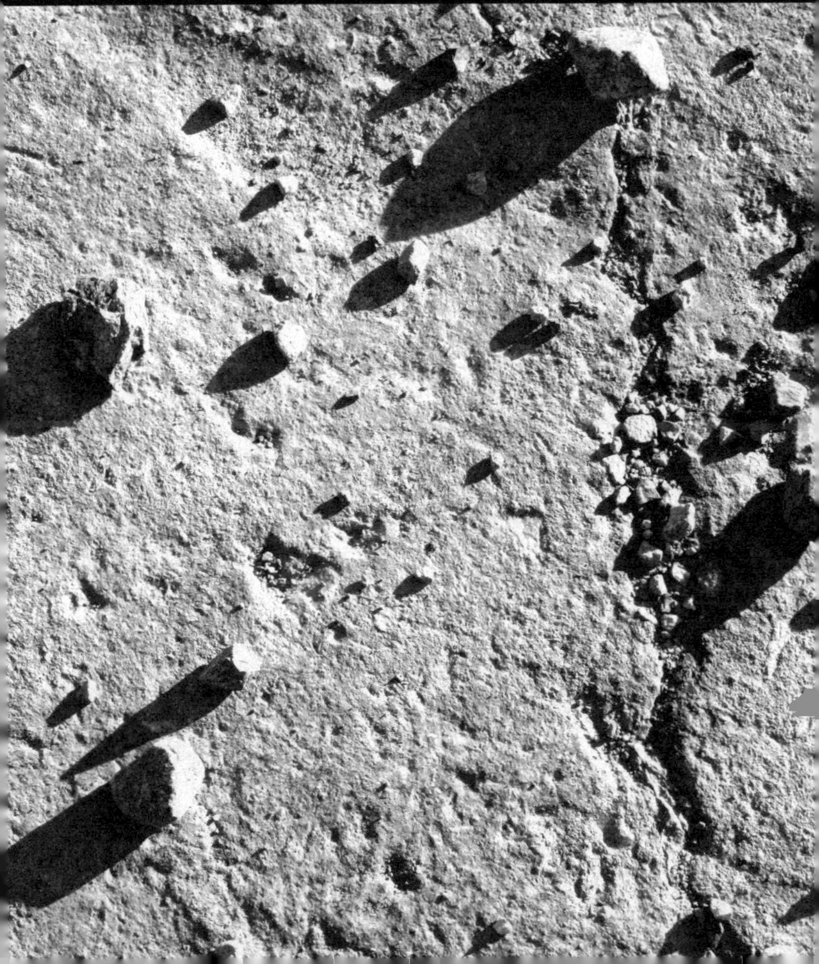

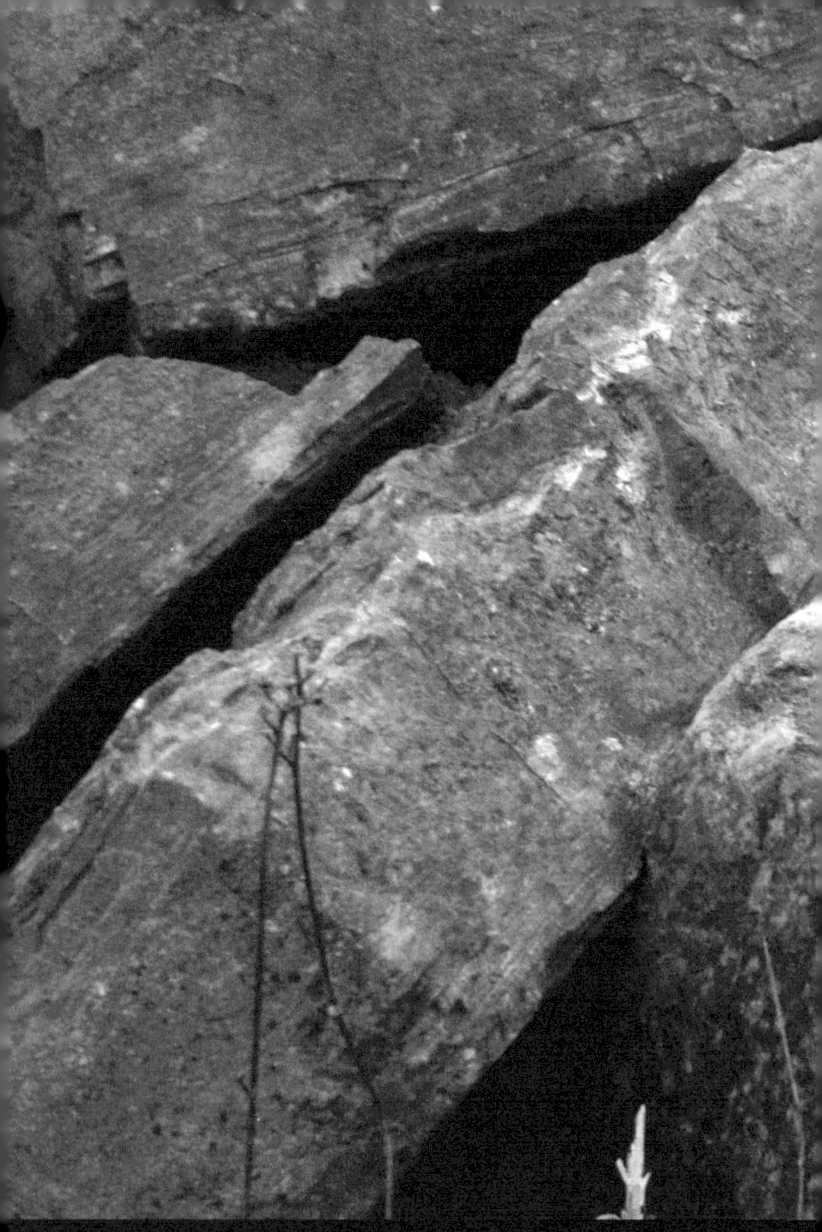

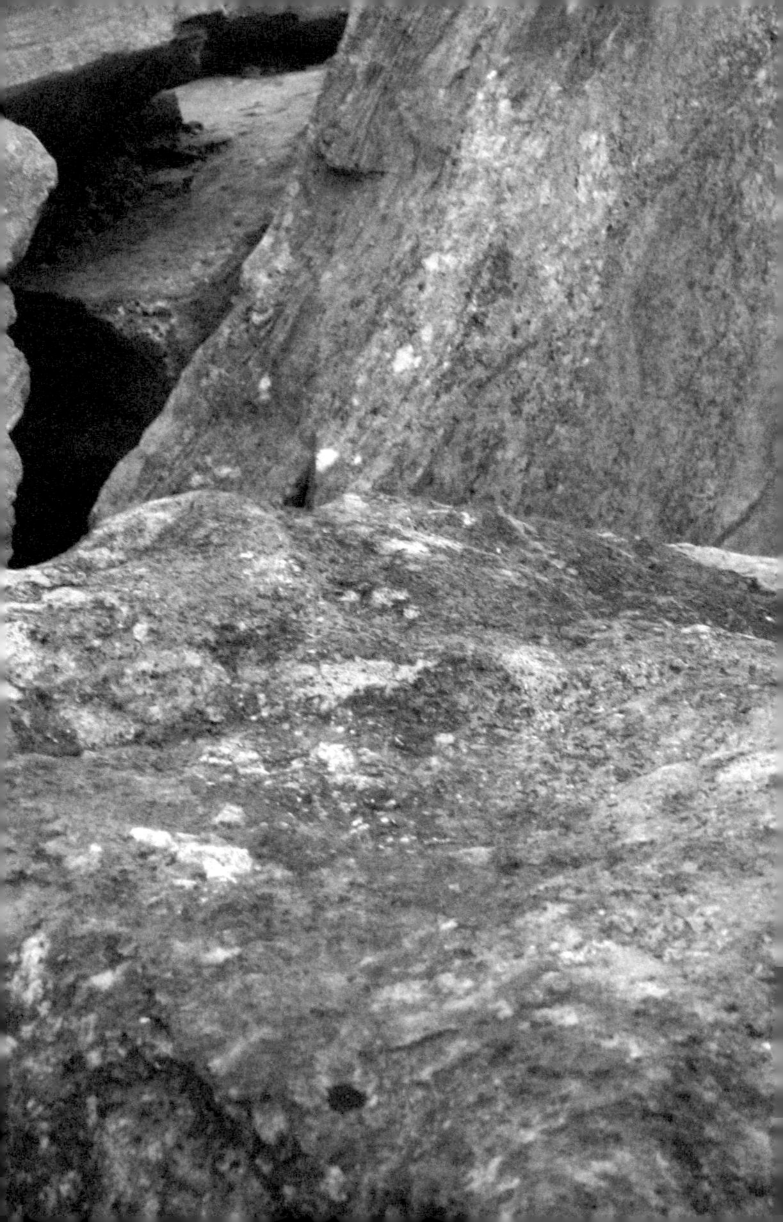

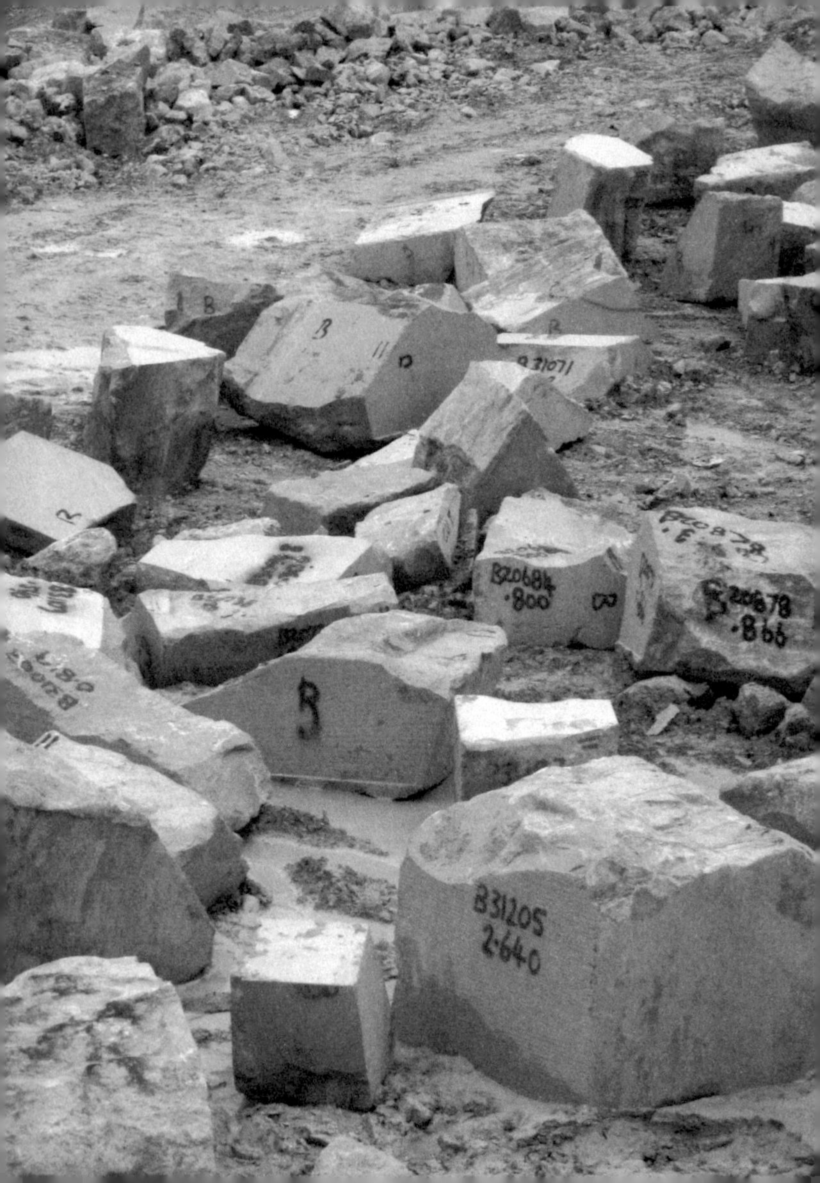
B31205
2·640
B20684
·800

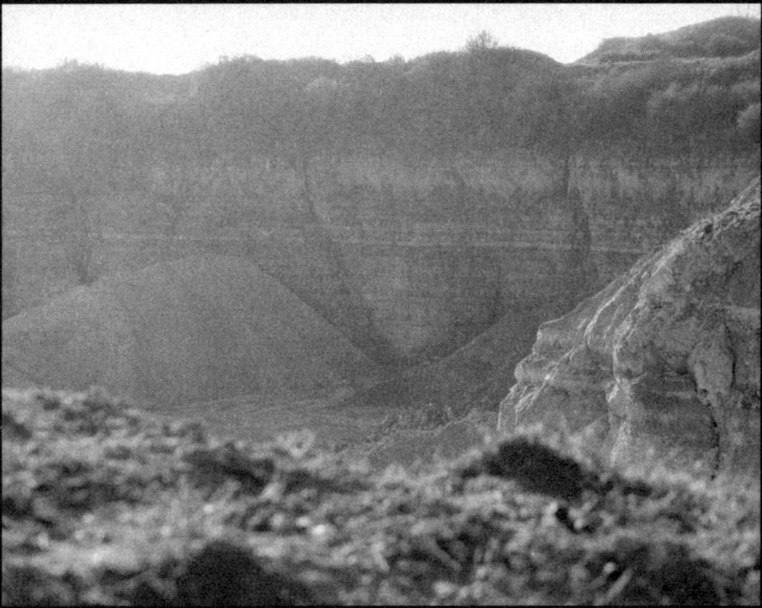

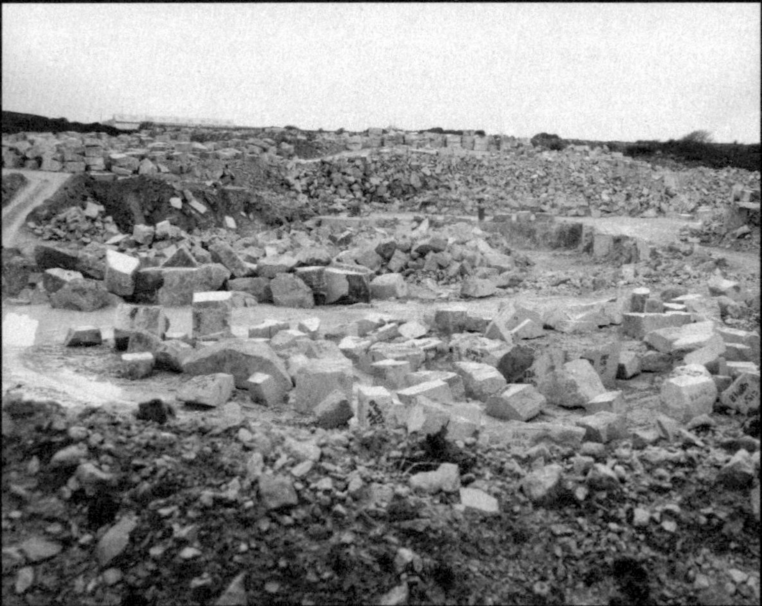

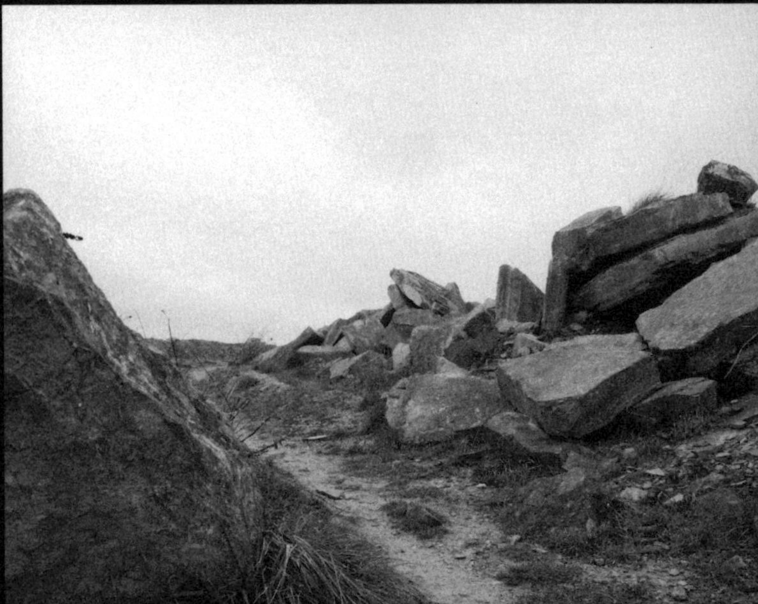

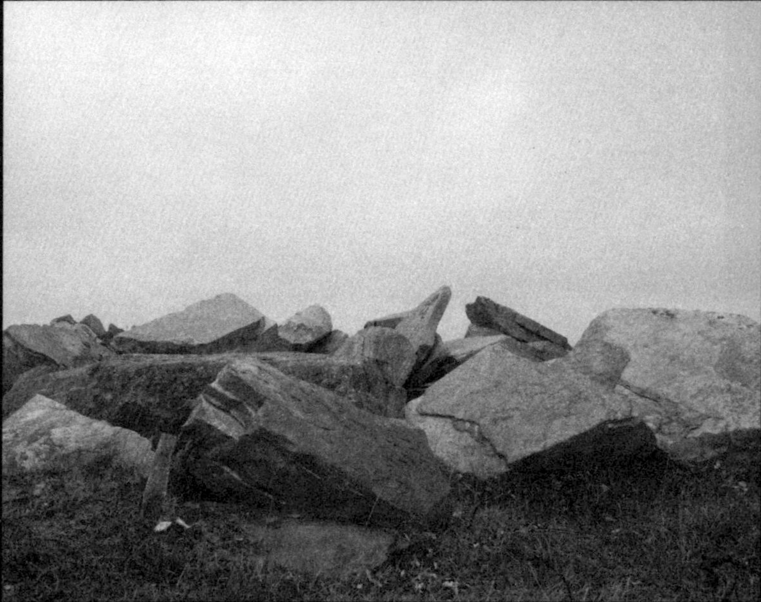

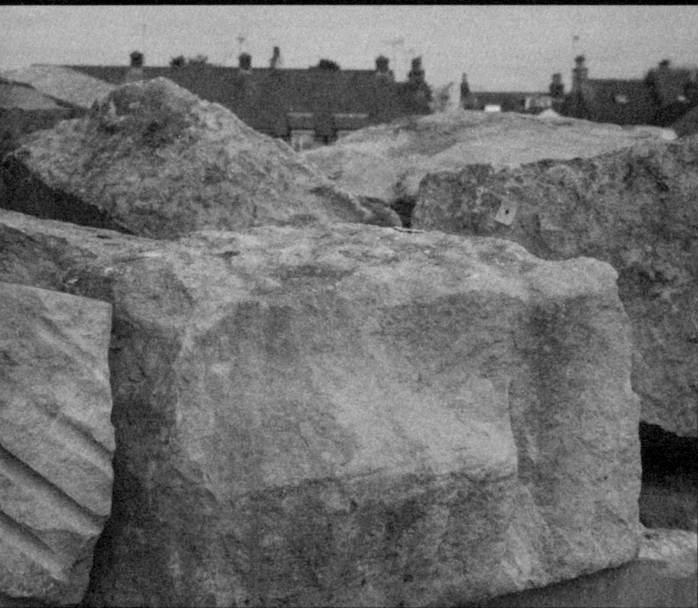

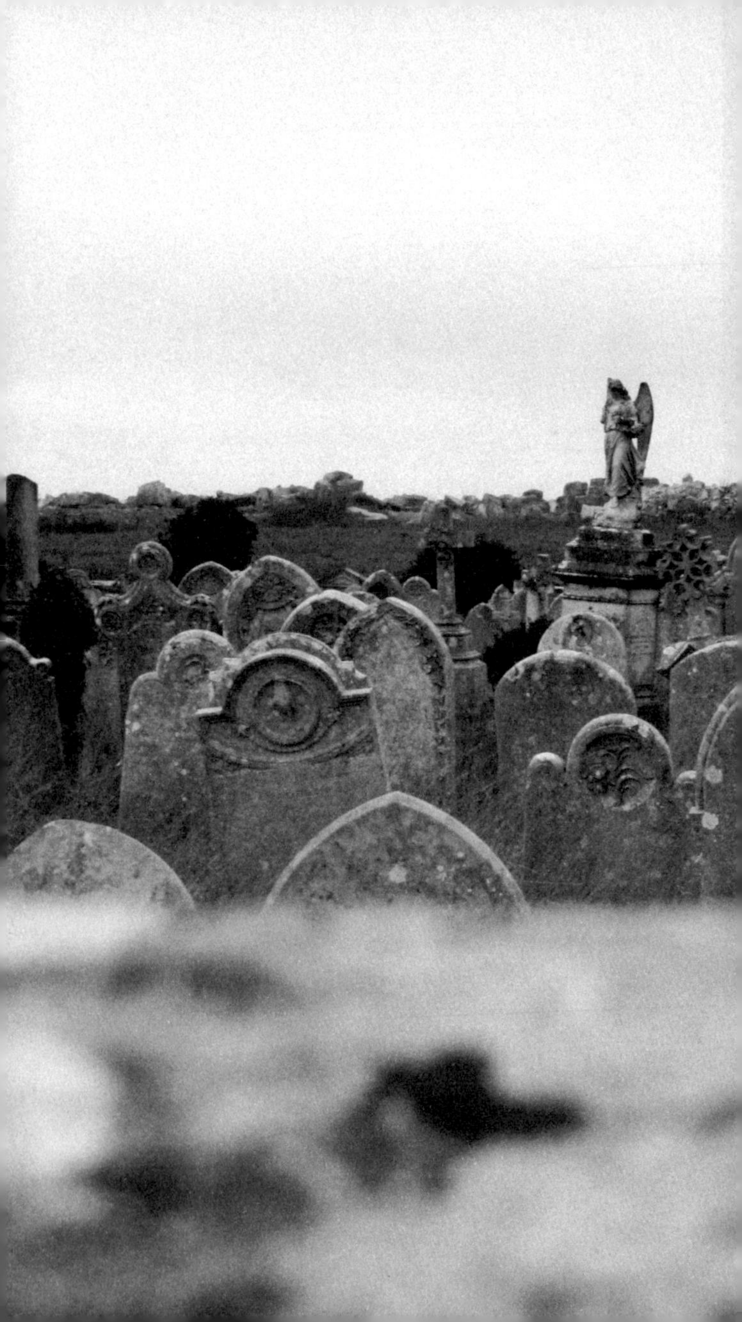

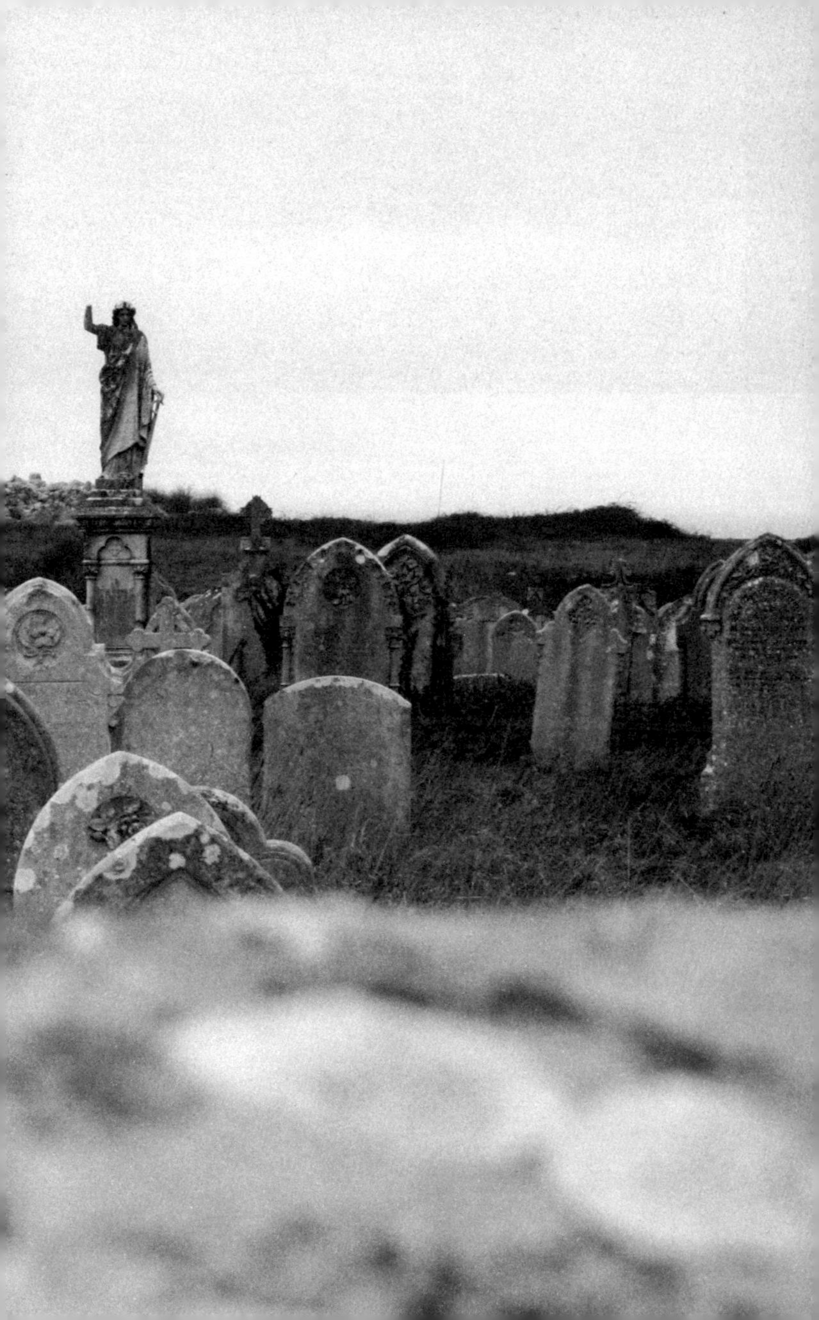

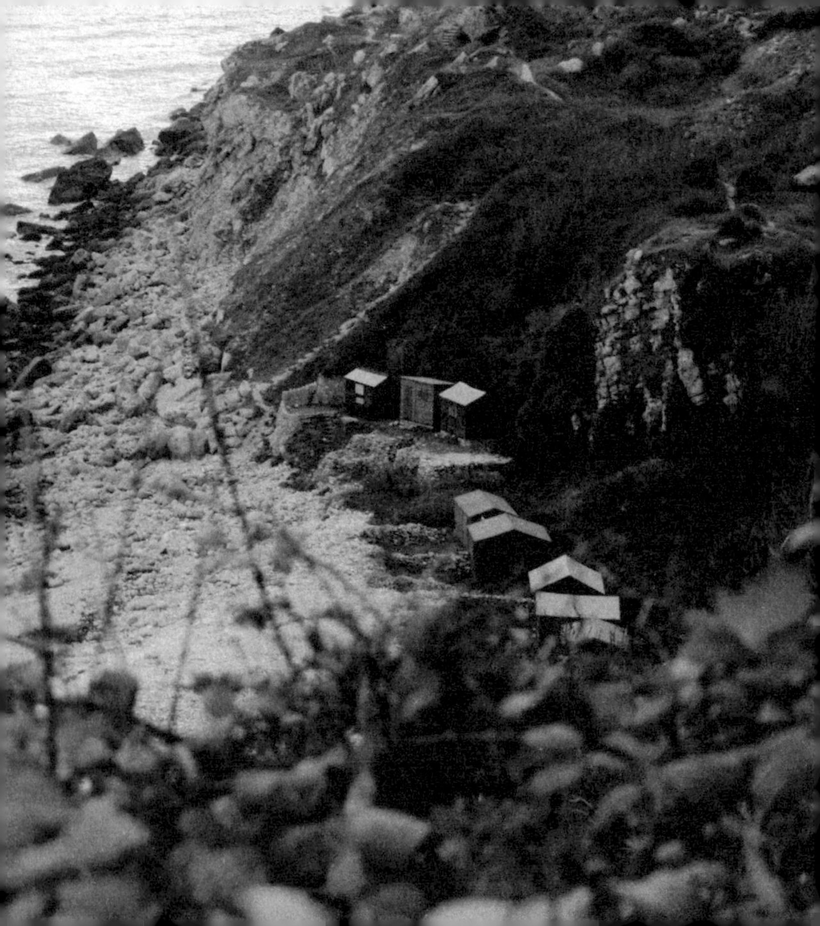

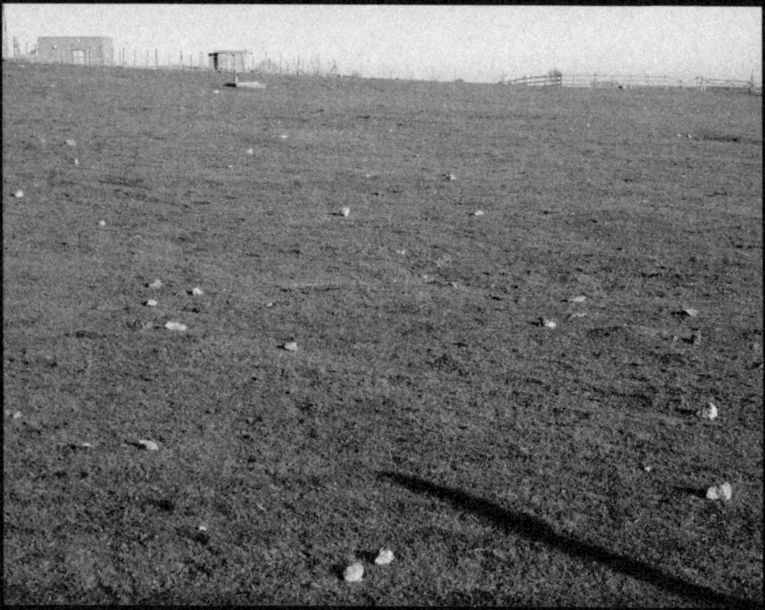

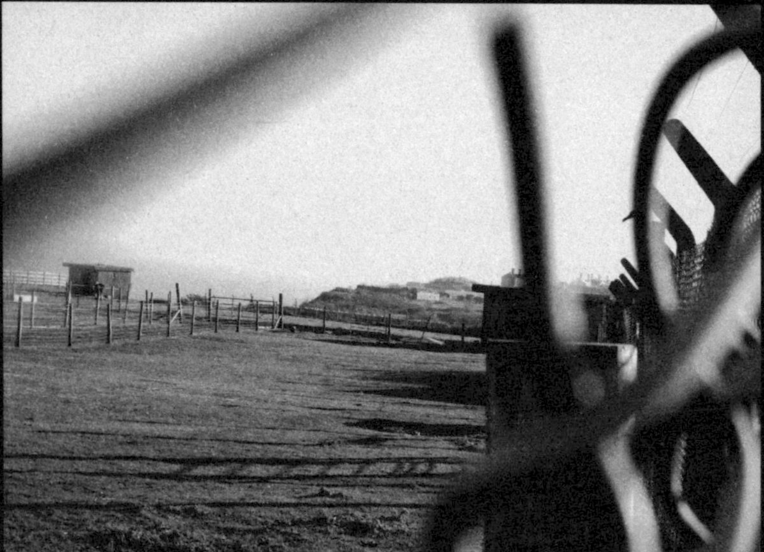

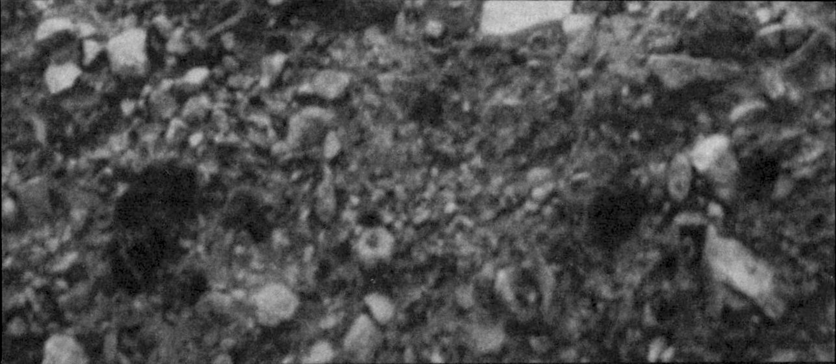

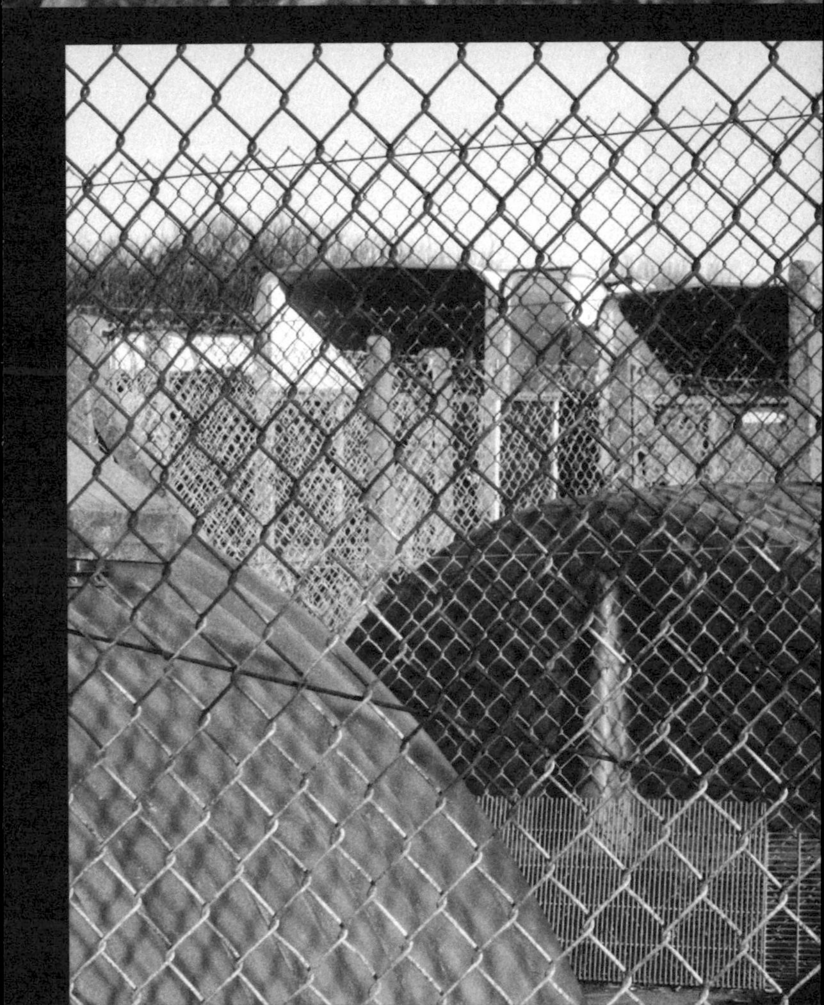

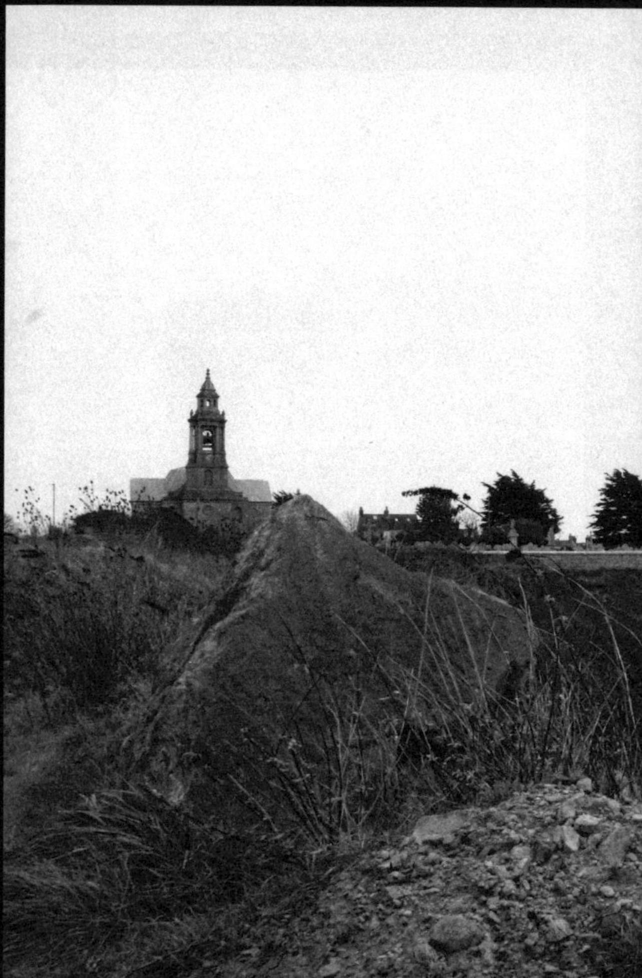

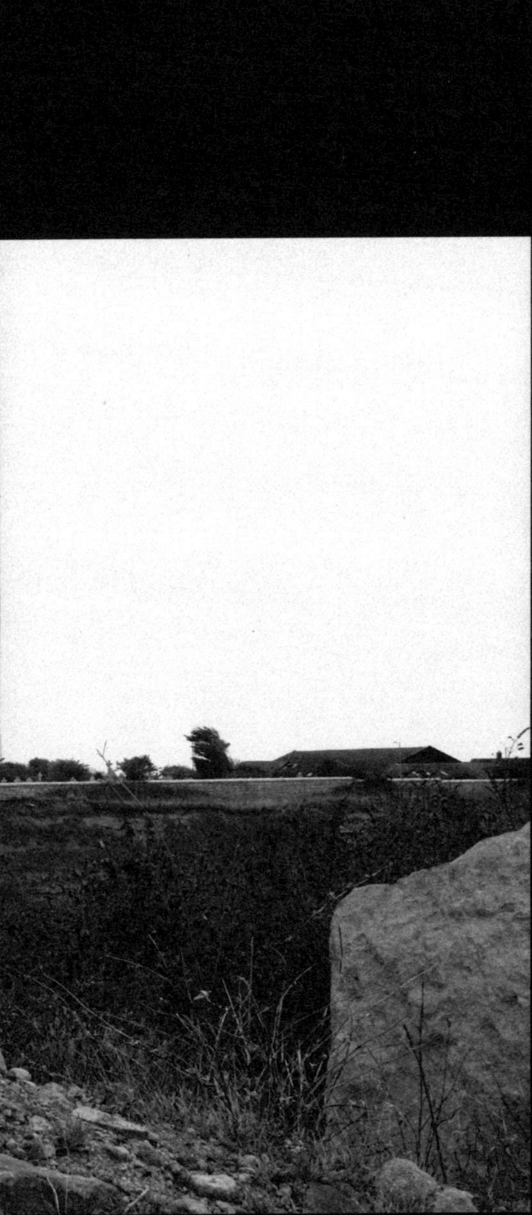

Epilogue

Besides the harrowing fate of the cats that used to be bricked into the stone walls of new houses for good luck, Portland's animals now thrive. If not existentially concerned with their own condition, they may be referred to as wordless witnesses, afforded special status by their proximity to the stone. The following animals live directly on its surface; balancing on its extremities, negotiating its open wounds and burrowing into its cavities.

The Goat

The wild goat featured in the story about Ash is one of a herd of rare English primitive goats. At the time of writing he continues to graze on the cliffside at Portland's East Weare.

The Horse

The horse that ran around Portland's entire coast was only witnessed by Miss Hazeline Horrocks of Church Ope Cove, and is still to be accounted for. Today Portland is a sanctuary for horses, but before the introduction of steam power to the quarries these animals were employed to move stone.

The Sheep

Fancy's Farm is home to the island's only flock of native sheep. Portland's golden-faced sheep are a rare breed, but since George III took a liking to it, their meat has had a reputation as a delicacy. The sheep disappeared from the island following the shrinkage of their grazing land due to quarrying. The few reared on the mainland ensured the breed's survival and they were initially reintroduced to the prison garden on Portland for a trial period in 1977. After a long period of being under threat, they were fought for, maintained and nurtured at Fancy's Farm, where they continue to flourish. The eccentric collection of buildings that the Farm currently occupies are the visible part of a redundant ROTOR radar station, constructed in 1951, as part of the UK's Cold War early-warning defence system. Today the sheep graze nonchalantly on the land that lies above the cavities of this station's extensive network of subterranean rooms and tunnels. Peculiar to their breed, they invariably only produce a single lamb.

The Pig

The pigs currently residing at Fancy's Farm do not bear any intentional resemblance to the pig that is depicted in this story and which subsequently died, following an episode of chronic indigestion.

The Rabbits

Many hundreds of rabbits continue to reside in Portland's shrubland and quarries. It is, however, considered unlucky to say the word 'rabbit' on Portland. Although the origin of this superstition is not confirmed, it has been suggested that it may be due to the historic frequency of landslides. A sighting of running rabbits would be an indicator of impending disaster.

Acknowledgements

End Matter is a commission by Artangel and BBC Radio 4.

The commission also includes *The Loss Adjusters*, produced by Artangel in association with b-side, presented on Portland in May/June 2015 with the support of The Henry Moore Foundation; and *The Quarryman's Daughters*, produced by Somethin' Else and broadcast on BBC Radio 4 in May 2015.

With thanks to Shaun Milton; Alex Borkowski, James Lingwood and Michael Morris, Artangel; Tony Phillips and Gwyneth Williams, BBC Radio 4; Gavin Everall, Jane Rolo, Book Works; James Langdon; Pattie Bolt, Portland Head Gardener and Gravedigger; Tony Booker, Albion Stone; Russell Finch and Joby Waldman, Somethin' Else; Tony Greaves; Chris Hammond, MOT International; Sandy Kirkby, Julie Penfold, Alan Rogers, Amanda Wallwork and Sally Watkins, b-side; Shirley Mitchell, Portland Heritage Centre.

Artangel is supported by Arts Council England
and The Company of Angels, Special Angels and Artangel International Circle
www.artangel.org.uk

Book Works receives National Portfolio Funding from
Arts Council England
www.bookworks.org.uk

End Matter by Katrina Palmer
Published by Artangel and Book Works
Distributed by Book Works
Co-Series: Book No. 9

Edited by Gavin Everall and James Lingwood
Proofread by Jacob Blandy
Designed by James Langdon
Printed by Die Keure, Belgium

ISBN 978 1 906012 73 1

Artangel

BOOK WORKS

Supported using public funding by ARTS COUNCIL ENGLAND

BBC RADIO 4